T0329702

WORKING IN A MULTICULTURAL WORLD:
A GUIDE TO DEVELOPING INTERCULTURAL
COMPETENCE

LUCIARA NARDON

Working
in a
Multicultural
World

A GUIDE TO DEVELOPING
INTERCULTURAL COMPETENCE

UNIVERSITY OF TORONTO PRESS
Toronto Buffalo London

© University of Toronto Press 2017
Rotman-UTP Publishing
Toronto Buffalo London
www.utorontopress.com

ISBN 978-1-4426-3728-3

Library and Archives Canada Cataloguing in Publication

Nardon, Luciara, 1972–, author
Working in a multicultural world : a guide to developing intercultural
competence/Luciara Nardon.

Includes bibliographical references and index.
ISBN 978-1-4426-3728-3 (cloth)

1. Intercultural communication. 2. Interpersonal communication.
3. Communication in organizations. 4. Work environment. I. Title.

HM1211.N37 2017   303.48'2   C2017-904416-8

University of Toronto Press acknowledges the financial assistance to its
publishing program of the Canada Council for the Arts and the Ontario Arts
Council, an agency of the Government of Ontario.

Canada Council   Conseil des Arts
for the Arts   du Canada

ONTARIO ARTS COUNCIL
CONSEIL DES ARTS DE L'ONTARIO
an Ontario government agency
un organisme du gouvernement de l'Ontario

Funded by the   Financé par le
Government gouvernement
of Canada   du Canada

To Ali and Caio

Contents

List of Figures

Acknowledgments

It takes a village to write a book! This book was only possible because of the support and input of many individuals throughout my life and career. *Working in a Multicultural World* emerged through my teaching of undergraduate and graduate students at Carleton University over the years. I am thankful for my students' questions, challenges, insights, and encouragement.

I am also thankful for my research collaborators' role in shaping my thinking and helping me develop the ideas that supported this book. I am thankful to Kathryn Aten, Diane Isabelle, and Betina Szkudlarek for the way our joint projects have shaped the direction of my work. I would like to offer special thanks to Richard Steers for his mentorship, support, and friendship over the years. This book was only possible because he was willing to teach me the art and craft of writing and research with patience and good cheer.

I am indebted to the many friends and research participants who have shared with me their intercultural stories over time. I am thankful for the research assistants Lisa Flick, Samuel Tersigni, and Leen Al-Jaber, who worked hard at different stages of this project and provided me with support and perceptive comments. I also would like to thank former student Michal Racek for a thoughtful reading of the first version of the manuscript and Anyi Ndongko for last-minute help with the figures.

I would like to specially acknowledge the work of the anonymous reviewers who provided incredibly insightful and detailed comments.

This work has grown significantly because of their insights. My editor at the University of Toronto Press, Jennifer DiDomenico, was instrumental in guiding this project through to completion by providing thoughtful and sensitive advice and support.

My son, Caio, has been a constant source of inspiration and encouragement. My husband, Ali, has read every single word of what I have written and has helped me find my way through this project with his infinite patience, kindness, and wisdom. They both have encouraged me when things were not going well and celebrated with me when things were moving along.

Thank you all for being a part of my life and for your contributions to making this book a reality.

Foreword

It is axiomatic that the more contacts we have with people from different countries and cultures, the greater the opportunities for increased learning and mutual understanding. This is a principal reason behind global work assignments, study abroad programs, international travel, community get-togethers, various interest groups, and even visits to local ethnic restaurants. Unfortunately, it does not follow that these interactions, however frequent or well-intentioned, will actually result in their desired outcomes. Preconceived ideas, prejudices, perceptual limitations, lack of experience, lack of attention, lack of curiosity, time constraints, and so forth, often inhibit our learning despite the opportunities we are presented with.

In this regard, the CEO of one of Europe's leading multinationals has observed that when multicultural teams sit and work together, the results can often be amazing, but that left on their own employees generally prefer to work with people from their own countries, and creativity can be lost. His conclusion: you often have to force people from different cultures to work together for their own (and the company's) good. In today's increasingly global environment, this pressure is now coming not so much from executives as from the work environment itself. Living and working across cultures is a global reality for an increasing number of people, foreign and domestic, in big cities and small, for majority populations and minorities. The trick is how to accomplish this.

Proximity is not the sole solution to this challenge, however. Getting people from different cultures to work together successfully requires two ingredients, not just one. People must have opportunities, but they also must have skills. They require opportunities to meet, interact, and share common experiences both inside and outside of work, however challenging these experiences may be for individuals who lack confidence in moving beyond their comfort zones. But people also require appropriate skill sets to provide them with the tools they need to succeed in strange, unique, and sometimes threatening encounters. To some extent, these skills are inborn, but for the most part they must be learned.

So, here is the dilemma: We are increasingly faced with situations both on the job and in our personal lives that require an increasing amount of intercultural competence, but many of us lack sufficient relevant skills to master these situations with both ease and effectiveness. As a result, opportunities are often lost. People interested in this dilemma will find the present volume to be a refreshingly candid – and insightful – examination of this topic. Not only does it explore the reasons underlying challenges to productive intercultural relations, but it goes further to suggest and illustrate several strategies for meeting these challenges.

The author, Luciara Nardon, begins this exploration with a series of basic questions that get to the heart of our daily personal and work experiences: How often do you interact with people from other cultures? How often do you expect to interact with other cultures in the future? Generally, how effective do you think you are in these interactions? And how often have you reflected upon your intercultural interactions and looked for better ways to respond? If these questions relate to your personal or work experiences, this is a volume you will wish to read carefully.

Luciara Nardon is uniquely qualified to explore this issue. Born and raised in Brazil, educated in Brazil, Argentina, and the United States, having worked in both North and South America, as well as in Europe and Asia, and now living and working in Canada, she brings a broad repertoire of multicultural industrial and academic experiences to her examination of how people process information and respond to intercultural interactions. She is widely published in our academic journals, serves on the editorial board of the *Journal of World Business*, has taught students and executives on four continents about working across cultural divides, and is the co-author of a leading text in the field, *Management across Cultures* (Cambridge University Press). She is also my former student and now my valued colleague.

Based on her research, Luciara argues that success in intercultural relations depends in no small part on a process of interaction that facilitates the development of common understandings and agreements about the norms governing interpersonal relations and creating a positive context. Context is a key word here, not just culture. Developing interpersonal competence requires both patience and practice. It is not a state where we withhold judgment or ignore negative emotions when interacting with people from other cultures. Instead, a knowledge of intercultural relations includes the skill to recognize when the thoughts and feelings we experience are not helping us to behave in ways that facilitate cooperation and understanding. Increased interpersonal competence allows us to engage with our own thoughts and feelings and to identify alternative courses of action that can lead to more successful interactions with others.

This book is organized around three principal themes: understanding the learning process associated with the development of intercultural competence; increasing awareness of relevant factors influencing intercultural interactions; and developing practical skills to interact more effectively. The book is rich in examples and draws heavily on reflective practice. It leads readers through a process of reflection about several concepts that are essential for developing intercultural competence. Each chapter presents a building block in developing this competence in some detail and ends with a reflective exercise for purposes of learning and skills application. The book is therefore both conceptual and practical, addressing both theory and application, and is certainly worth studying.

It has been said that the world is not getting smaller, it is getting faster. If this is true, our ability to keep up – to survive and to succeed – depends on our capacity for continual growth and development in both our work and personal lives. *Working in a Multicultural World* is a useful tool in this development.

Richard M. Steers
University of Oregon, U.S.A.

Preface

I have been thinking about writing this book since my early years as an international student in the United States. As a graduate student, I was very interested in my international management courses and devoured multiple books on culture and behavior in an effort to understand what made me both different from and similar to my classmates, and to find solutions to the many difficulties associated with adjusting to a foreign cultural environment. However, something about the approach of explaining cultural differences and categorizing cultural groups did not work for me. I cringed when my behavior was labeled as "Brazilian" or, even worse, when I was told I did *not* behave "Brazilian." Back then, I longed for a more comprehensive and inclusive explanation of behavior in intercultural situations and a method for developing my intercultural competence that went beyond acquiring knowledge of other cultures.

It has taken me about two decades to be able to understand and articulate what I see as the main forces guiding an intercultural situation and, building on a wide literature, to develop a method for intercultural learning for myself and my students. The process that I propose in this book rests on the assumption that knowledge of other cultures, while helpful, is insufficient. At some point in time, the knowledge we have will not apply to the context we are in, or it will be incomplete, wrong, or oversimplified. Instead of focusing on cultural knowledge, I propose a focus on the *process of intercultural interactions* and increased self- and situational awareness.

Focusing on a process is not easy, though. A process is not as tangible and demarcated as a piece of information. It is much easier to convey and accept notions such as "The Chinese value relationships" than it is to rely on a process to build a positive relationship with a Chinese person. However, while the former may feel more comfortable, it is the latter that will result in more sustainable benefits.

While this book focuses on intercultural interactions, often the situations I describe could happen between individuals of the same community. As I discuss in chapter four, individuals belong to multiple cultures, some of which may be small in size and scope (e.g., a departmental culture), and many *interpersonal* interactions can be understood through cultural lenses. As you think about your own intercultural experiences, consider them broadly and do not restrict yourself to situations in which multiple nationalities are involved.

Most of the examples in this book were based on stories reported to me by colleagues, students, or informants during my research. I have modified the details of their stories to preserve their anonymity but have not changed their country of origin and gender. I avoided hypothetical examples, as they do not have the reflective nature I am after. Any bias in representation is accidental and representative of the groups in which I was involved at the time of this work.

Throughout the book, I refer to individuals as "him" or "her" at random.

How to Use This Book

This book draws heavily on reflective practice. I have practiced reflective journaling daily for almost twenty years. I started a journal after I read Julia Cameron's *The Artist's Way*[1] and was intrigued by the idea of *morning pages*, a daily ritual of writing by hand whatever comes to mind upon waking as a tool to increase creativity. As I started to appreciate the journaling experience, I began to explore the literature on reflective practice and experiment with more structured approaches to writing and reflecting. Reflective practice grew on me and became the primary mechanism through which I make sense of issues, soothe my emotions, and plan for the future. It was this practice that helped me deal with the many intercultural issues I faced in my international life and career and that supported the process of writing this book.

This book will guide you through a process of reflection on key concepts essential for the development of intercultural competence. In each chapter, I discuss a key building block of intercultural competence in detail, and suggest a reflective exercise. These exercises are designed to help you deepen your understanding of and integrate the concepts discussed in the chapter. As such, it is best to read this book slowly, taking the time to reflect on each concept and explore its significance for your own life. It is also a good idea to have a notebook close by in which to record your thoughts and feelings as you work through the concepts presented here.

The reflective exercises presented in this book have evolved through multiple rounds of revision as readers asked for more clarity, more structure, and more consistency. As a result, the exercises are tailored for those who thrive on structure, though they may feel stifling for others who are more comfortable with the process of reflection. Personally, I approach my reflections in an unstructured and nonlinear way. I enjoy the freedom of free writing and tend to follow my mind first and then look back and consider where it has been. As Karl Weick and colleagues suggest, "How do I know what I think, until I see what I say?"[2] However, as I started using reflective exercises in the classroom, I realized that while some individuals are fond of reflections and comfortable with a free flow of ideas, others need more guidance. My recommendation is that you start by free writing, describing your experience based on what is salient to you, and fill in missing details based on the questions proposed in a second round of writing. I encourage you to experiment with the process and find what works best for you.

Even though following the structured questions is optional, my personal and classroom experience suggests that *revisiting* the reflections is critical (step 2, as discussed in chapter 2). In the first round of reflection, the telling of the story is often emotionally charged (he did that to me and I don't like it), the theories of behavior are highly biased (he is so selfish), and the conclusions are often not helpful (I'd rather not work with him again). It is in the *revisiting*, once the emotions have calmed, and through a more deliberate process of evaluation that the insights arise (I had a role to play in this situation). It is difficult to predict how much time needs to pass between writing and revisiting a story, as it depends on how emotionally charged the situation is and how open we are to (re)-evaluate it – from a few minutes to several days. If, as you start revisiting your reflection, you still feel emotional about the situation, it may be a good idea to wait a little longer before revisiting it.

Most exercises ask you to consider a recent intercultural interaction followed by a set of guiding questions. The basic reflection process is discussed in detail in chapter 2 and repeated in subsequent chapters. In addition to the basic questions, each exercise invites a deeper reflection on the concepts discussed in the chapter. Depending on your needs and circumstances, you may choose to reflect upon different situations each time, repeating the basic reflective process, and exploring the concepts discussed in the chapter. This approach works best if you do not have a specific challenge in mind and are looking for a general understanding of intercultural interactions. As an alternative, you might focus on one main situation throughout the book, revisiting it repeatedly and adding more details and richness at each reflective round. This method works particularly well if you are grappling with an important issue (e.g., trying to improve your relationship with a co-worker from another culture). For the convenience of those working with multiple reflections, general questions are repeated every time. Readers using the reflective exercises to deepen their understanding of one situation may focus on the new questions. For ease of identification, repeated questions are signaled with a check mark.

The developmental model presented here assumes that you have a desire to improve your intercultural skills and a willingness to engage in the process. You need to accept the vulnerability associated with questioning yourself and tolerate the ambiguity associated with a process that does not bring immediate tangible answers. Further, reading a book is often a lonely process, but intercultural interactions are not. If you are reading this book on your own, you will benefit from engaging in dialogue with others in order to deepen your insights and validate your learning.

Using This Book in the Classroom

Even though this book was not conceived as a textbook, I have used the concepts and exercises proposed in this book in MBA courses on International Management as a complement to case studies for both experienced and inexperienced students.

When teaching inexperienced students, I provide them with opportunities for intercultural experiences (usually weekly) within the university or the community. Depending on the makeup of the class, I may place students in multicultural teams or organize intercultural activities outside the classroom. In this case, I require students to *write their stories* weekly after their experience, and *revisit* their stories in the middle and at the end of the academic term. Throughout the term, I provide them with detailed feedback, asking questions and encouraging them to deepen their reflection. For experienced students, typically taught in compressed class schedules, I ask students to focus on one work situation and revisit it once, including all concepts discussed in the course. A compressed reflection exercise including all concepts is presented in appendix B.

Overview of the Book

This book is organized around three main themes: understanding the learning process associated with the development of intercultural competence (chapters 1 and 2); increasing awareness of relevant factors influencing intercultural interactions (chapters 3, 4, and 5); and developing practical skills to interact more effectively (chapters 7,

8, and 9). These themes are interrelated in the real-life experience of intercultural interactions, but for readability are introduced one at a time.

Chapter 1 introduces the challenges and benefits of intercultural interactions and the role of intercultural competence in helping us make the most of multicultural workplaces. It explores how mental models are developed and how they influence the ways we see the world and react to situations and discusses how intercultural competence depends on effective mental models that include appropriate ways of thinking and behaving in intercultural situations.

Chapter 2 presents reflection as a mechanism to develop and expand intercultural mental models and develop intercultural competence. It elaborates on the four steps of the reflective process (tell story, revisit story, prepare for the future, apply learning) and provides suggestions for making the most of a reflective practice. It also discusses the path toward being reflective, our ultimate goal.

Chapter 3 discusses the situated nature of intercultural interactions and explores the role of culture, individual characteristics, situational context, and behavior in shaping intercultural interactions. It introduces the process of intercultural sensemaking and the need for situational awareness.

Chapter 4 focuses on the role of culture in influencing behavior in intercultural interactions. It explores how behavior is influenced by culture differently within and across cultures, and across situations. It proposes cultural self-awareness as a mechanism to compensate for lack of knowledge of other cultures and to provide guidance regarding how to behave in intercultural situations.

Chapter 5 discusses individual characteristics and their influence in intercultural interactions. Individual characteristics influence the degree to which individuals subscribe to their cultures, their ability to overcome cultural limitations, and their sensitivity to contextual cues. The chapter also discusses the role of managing identities and self-awareness in facilitating the development of intercultural competence.

Chapter 6 revisits the role of situations and focuses on the immediate context surrounding an interaction, including situational strength, role expectations, and physical setting. Further, it elaborates on our own role in shaping the situations in which we are immersed.

Chapter 7 explores the role of managing feelings in the development of intercultural competence. Intercultural interactions have the potential to elicit both positive and negative feelings, which influence the way we think and act. The chapter highlights the importance of emotional awareness in intercultural interactions, discusses the relationship between culture and feelings, proposes avenues for working with feelings, and discusses the importance of empathy in intercultural interactions.

Chapter 8 discusses the process of creating a shared understanding through communication. It looks at the role of culture in shaping how we communicate and proposes communication mechanisms to facilitate understanding and avenues for managing intercultural conflicts.

Chapter 9 integrates the concepts discussed throughout the book and provides guidelines for intercultural relations. It also discusses avenues for continuous development of intercultural competence, including how to engage in intercultural experiences for learning and how to learn from secondary information.

WORKING IN A MULTICULTURAL WORLD:
A GUIDE TO DEVELOPING INTERCULTURAL
COMPETENCE

CHAPTER 1

Working in a Multicultural World

Speak in French when you can't think of the English for a thing – turn your toes out when you walk – and remember who you are!

Lewis Carroll, *Through the Looking-Glass*

We no longer need to fall into the rabbit hole or go through the looking glass to experience the wonderland of meeting different people with unexpected behaviors. This week alone I have dealt with people from at least twenty different cultures. Today, I had a departmental meeting at work: five people, five countries, and four continents were represented. Later, I went on to teach my MBA course. Out of a group of twenty-five students, only five self-identified as Canadians, whereas the others were international students from a variety of places. After class, I met with my doctoral student from Poland, had a conference call with co-authors from Greece and the United States, and met a Turkish woman to discuss a potential new project. And I am not even counting that I came home to an Iranian husband, a Canadian child, and a Brazilian mother.

I am not alone. Laura, a top finance executive in a large Brazilian manufacturing firm, works closely with peers and subordinates across eight different countries – in person and virtually. Peter, a sales executive in a large Belgian service organization, travels abroad an average of 250 days every year. Dorothy, a training and development manager in a Canadian health-care organization, is responsible for training and integrating professional migrant workers and works with twenty to thirty individuals from different countries and cultures every year. For us, and for many others, interacting with people from other cultures is an essential part of life.

If you picked up this book, you are likely concerned with how to get the most out of your intercultural experiences. Like many of us, your work performance may depend on your ability to interact successfully with people from other cultures. Whether we are negotiating with international partners, serving a diverse customer base, managing a multicultural team, or simply working in a multicultural environment, most of us are faced with intercultural situations on a regular basis.

It is estimated that there are 232 million migrants[1] and more than 50 million expatriates[2] worldwide. As a result, our societies and organizations are becoming increasingly diverse. In addition, many of us may travel or deal with travelers on short-term assignments and interact virtually with others located in other cultures. It quickly becomes clear that intercultural encounters are a pervasive feature of our modern workplaces and affect most of us. This book is aimed at *helping you develop constructive ways of thinking about intercultural interactions and acquire the skills needed to deal with the complex multicultural reality of today's workplace.*

Think for a moment: How often do you interact with people from other cultures? How often do you expect to interact with people from other cultures in the future? Consider the intercultural interactions you had in the past. How effective do you think you were in these interactions? How often do you reflect upon your intercultural interactions and look for better ways to interact?

The Challenges and Benefits of Intercultural Interactions

Intercultural interactions have the potential to create synergies and bring many benefits to organizations and individuals. For instance, research in organizational diversity suggests that a diverse work-force can bring many benefits to organizations because employees have access to diverse information, knowledge, and perspectives. Multicultural teams are often more creative in developing ideas and solutions and often more knowledgeable about global markets and more effective in dealing with international customers and employ-ees when compared with culturally homogeneous teams.[3] Inter-cultural interactions also bring many benefits to individuals. When we interact with people from other cultures we can learn more about the world around us and, more importantly, learn more about our-selves. By being exposed to other points of view, we can develop a better understanding of why we think the way we do – and of our own behavior – and perhaps change for the better.

However, developing successful relationships with people from different cultures can also present us with some challenges. Several reasons account for this, such as our tendency to have preconceived notions about how the world works (or should work), how indi-viduals behave (or should behave), and which behaviors are accept-able (or unacceptable). These ideas are largely influenced by our personal experiences and the cultures in which we grew up. If we are not mindful, we may approach intercultural interactions based on our own perceptions, beliefs, values, biases, and assumptions about what is likely to happen. As a result, when we work with people from different cultures, we may find that the consequences of our actions are quite different from the ones we anticipated.

Management researchers often refer to cultural diversity as a double-edged sword.[4] Despite the many benefits of interacting with people with different values, beliefs, and assumptions, the same di-versity that brings in new perspectives also increases opportunities for conflict, disagreements, and misunderstandings. Getting things done often takes longer than anticipated, as we need to work through many different ideas and decision-making styles. Communication processes are more demanding than in monocultural situations, as many assumptions need to be articulated and explained, messages are often unclear or difficult to interpret, and important pieces of information can get lost. It may be difficult to establish rapport, find areas of common interest, and develop trust. And opportunities for conflict abound: we think differently, we value different things, and we have different beliefs and assumptions about how the world works, about the specific issues at hand, and about how to go about dealing with them.

It is not surprising, then, that we are naturally attracted to people who are like us, and find it easier to work with people who see the world the same way we do. As Atsushi Kagayama from Panasonic Corporation once said, "Getting Americans and Japanese to work together is like mixing hamburger with sushi."[5] My experience with diverse groups in the classroom is that if I let students choose who they want to work with, they quickly navigate toward people like themselves and form homogeneous teams. However, when they are forced into multicultural teams they usually report learning and benefiting from the experience. As one student reflected, "When I first learned about this assignment, I really had questions about what I would gain from this experience ... however [after several meetings and discussions and seeing things] from a completely different perspective, I understand the value added ..."

Intercultural Encounters and Ambiguity

One of the key challenges of intercultural encounters is that they are inherently ambiguous. *Intercultural encounters* are meetings or interactions, often unplanned or unexpected, with individuals from other cultural groups. They are inherently ambiguous because the cultural rules and their role in shaping people's behavior are not clear. Consequently, we may not know how to behave, and we can't predict how things will turn out. This ambiguity is not necessarily a bad thing. Consider the following situations:

- *Many intercultural encounters happen on short notice, leaving little time to learn about the other culture.* Imagine that you have just returned from a week's stay in India where you were negotiating an outsourcing agreement. As you arrive in your home office, you learn that an outsourcing opportunity just turned up in Honduras and that you are supposed to leave in a week to further explore the matter. You have never been to Honduras, nor do you know anybody from there. What do you do?

- *There is often more than one culture involved in an interaction, and it is not always clear how each one plays out or is dominant in a situation.* You arrive in Honduras to negotiate the agreement and find out you are negotiating a contract with a Saudi manager working for a French company in Honduras. Learning about Saudi, French, and Honduran cultures, while useful, still leaves us with limited understanding of what to do in the current situation. Is it the Saudi cultural background of the individual, the company culture, which may be influenced by the French business culture, or the local Honduran culture where the interaction takes place that determines appropriate – and inappropriate – behaviors? Alternatively, suppose your company has asked you to join a global research team. The team includes people from Mexico, Germany, China, and Russia, all of whom have a permanent appointment in their home country but have been temporarily assigned to work on this project at company headquarters in Switzerland. The group members must be able to work together quickly and effectively to produce results, despite their differences. What do you do?

- *People often behave differently when interacting across cultures.* Think about it: While you are trying to figure out how to deal with your Saudi counterpart and are adjusting your behavior as best you can, what do you think your counterpart is doing? The same thing. People automatically adjust their behavior when dealing with people from other cultures. This adjustment does not necessarily make things easier or increase cultural fit; rather, it often makes situations more ambiguous because it is not clear if the behavior we are seeing is a product of a cultural background or an attempt to adjust to another culture. Again, what do you do?

In each of these situations, there are cultural differences to be dealt with, but it is not clear how these differences will play out. *Cross-cultural knowledge*, or the knowledge of how behaviors are different across cultural groups, while helpful, is insufficient. That is, knowing how Saudis behave while in Saudi Arabia may help us understand some behaviors but does not offer guidelines regarding how to behave in this specific situation of negotiating with the Saudi manager in Honduras. Just as Lewis Carroll's Alice found (see the introductory quotation) when encountering the new world of the looking glass, learning the *dos* and *don'ts* of other cultures is of little help in ambiguous situations. First, simplistic cultural rules do not account for the fact that each intercultural situation is unique – it involves different people, contexts, and dynamics and requires different actions and reactions. Second, cultural rules do not account for how you personally may have changed the situation and altered the expectations of others involved. In these situations, we need *intercultural competence* – mental and behavioral skills related to the *process* of working or interacting with people from other cultures. Intercultural competence is manifested in ways of thinking and behaving that allow us to work with others who are different from us, for all parties' mutual benefit, in situations in which it is not clear what the cultural rules are.

Intercultural Competence

We are cultural beings. Through socialization in a cultural community, we acquire a collection of perspectives, beliefs, values, assumptions, worldviews, habits, and ways of life that influence our attitudes and behaviors in ways that we are often unaware of. Culture constrains our behavior by providing limits around what is considered acceptable and by providing us with habits and skills that shape how we behave. The hallmark of *cultural competence* is the ability to *behave in culturally appropriate ways instinctively*, something we all do within cultural groups in which we have spent a significant amount of time and which we understand.

However, in an intercultural interaction, our habitual and readily available behaviors may not be effective or desirable, and our values, beliefs, and assumptions may not be shared. When interacting interculturally, we must be able to suspend our automatic behavior to act more appropriately. *Intercultural competence* is the ability to overcome the constraints imposed by our natural cultural tendencies and develop new responses.[6] As such, intercultural competence is more than cultural knowledge; it is the ability to *behave in ways that facilitate understanding* – regardless of how much knowledge we have of a certain culture.[7] Let's consider the differences between cultural knowledge, cultural competence, and intercultural competence with an example. You may have heard or observed the custom of Arab people to greet one another with cheek-to-cheek kisses. This information is *cultural knowledge*. However, a more detailed understanding of whom-to-kiss-when and the ability to perceive the nuances of situations and their implications with regard to kissing is *cultural competence*. *Intercultural competence*, on the other hand, is the ability to navigate a situation even when you are not sure if kissing is called for or not. Intercultural competence may manifest itself through careful observation, a clear statement of the norms in place, or perhaps simply the ability to articulate one's confusion and ask for guidance.

At first, intercultural interactions require us to suspend automatic cultural responses and try new, alternative behaviors. Over time, these newly learned responses will become part of our repertoire of behavior and may be called into action effortlessly. However, during the intercultural learning process, these new behaviors may require concentrated attention and effort to acquire, both during and after intercultural interactions. We now turn to the *process* of intercultural learning.

Intercultural Learning

Transformative learning is a theory of adult learning particularly well suited to help us understand the process of intercultural learning and the development of intercultural competence.[8] According to transformative learning theory, learning is a process of revising our mental models that results in changes in our interpretation of experience and action.

Mental Models

A *mental model* is a picture in our mind of how the world works.[9] We reason by constructing mental models of a situation.[10] As we experience a situation, these mental models allow for the development of tentative conclusions, which we test by trying to build counter-examples in which the conclusion might be false. The conclusion is assumed to be correct if no counter-examples can be found. Mental models help us make sense of the world around us and tell us how to behave in different situations. For example, when you think of a "birthday party," you call to mind a complex image of what a birthday party looks like, including your expectations around key artifacts (e.g., birthday cake, candles, gifts), behaviors (e.g., singing "Happy Birthday," gift giving), and meanings (e.g., blowing out candles). Mental models are abstractions we make of the world that help us quickly incorporate information, figure out what is important and requires our attention, and simplify our experiences. We are largely unaware of our mental models, as they are often below our level of conscious awareness and do not require any deliberate thought.

We are constantly bombarded with bits of sensory information as we experience the world, and we rely on our mental models to make quick leaps from particulars to general concepts. For example, if when we arrive at the office we see a cake in the staff lunchroom, we may quickly jump to the conclusion that it is somebody's birthday and ask, "Whose birthday is it today?" Mental models simplify our lives and decrease the cognitive energy needed to make sense of the world around us. They are shortcuts that allow us to make sense of things quickly and guide our actions. Mental models are very helpful, as they allow us to move through the world quickly, recognize dangers and opportunities, and know how to act in a given situation. We do not have time to ponder what to do when we are standing in front of a bear; we rely on our mental models to decide how to react.

Mental models are developed through our life experiences and, consequently, are heavily influenced by our cultural environment. We acquire our mental models *uncritically* and are often unaware of how we came to think the way we do and the biases we may have.

Mental models are necessary to organize our experience and facilitate everyday actions, but at the same time they distort our perceptions of reality by operating as *filters*, which we use to see the world. The less exposed we are to different cultures, the more likely we are to have mental models based on a limited set of assumptions and worldviews. Thus, intercultural learning, to be useful, needs to be *transformative* because it involves a *critical reassessment* of assumptions, beliefs, and premises embedded in our mental models.

Experience and Learning

Experience has long been recognized as an important component in learning in general and in intercultural learning in particular. Sending people abroad is a well-known strategy employed by organizations and academic institutions with the aim of developing employees' and students' intercultural competence. Despite the critical role of experience in developing intercultural skills, recent studies show that international or intercultural experiences do not always result in learning[11] and suggest that just sending people abroad is insufficient for the development of intercultural competence.[12] People may even go abroad and come back more attached to their own cultural views than ever, rather than learning how to deal with other points of view and developing new and more inclusive perspectives. For example, a person going to India and experiencing bargaining at a street market may regard the experience as amusing but may not change his thinking or behavior about the practice. Worse, he may regard his own culture as superior and develop stronger ethnocentric views than he may have had before the experience.

A critical step in transforming experience and developing intercultural competence is the desire and ability of individuals to make sense of experienced discrepancies through self-reflection and to incorporate the learning into their mental models. To learn from experience, it is necessary to make sense of what has happened; to understand the causes of problems, the strategies that worked, and the ones that didn't; and, more importantly, to understand why things turned out the way they did. In other words, we need more than just first-hand experience of other cultures. To develop intercultural competence, we need to think about what has happened with an open mind, consider its causes and outcomes, and identify implications for future behavior. This process is illustrated in figure 1.1. The next chapter discusses the role of reflection in the development of intercultural mental models.

Stages in Intercultural Development

Working in multicultural settings requires a sophisticated mental model that includes a repertoire of thinking processes and behaviors that will help us navigate ambiguous and dynamic intercultural situations. This intercultural mental model allows us to consider, during an intercultural interaction, the demands and constraints of the specific situation, the expectations of others, and our own and others' motives and goals, in order to choose the behaviors that are most appropriate for that situation.

Mental models are dynamic and evolve over time. Research suggests that people's mental models evolve over time in three stages: at first, we employ naive models that are simplified and draw primarily on hunches and commonsense. As we gain familiarity with our domain, we develop some explicit models and become more careful observers, eventually developing a sophisticated mental model that is significantly more complex and nuanced.[13] Drawing on this body of work, we can extrapolate a model of intercultural development as illustrated in table 1.1 and explained below. I start by describing each mental model and then discussing avenues for development.

A Monocultural Mental Model

Individuals with a *monocultural mental model* are largely unaware of cross-cultural differences. Their own cultural assumptions, values, and beliefs are taken for granted. They may hold a few general stereotypes about other cultures and rely on their own cultural

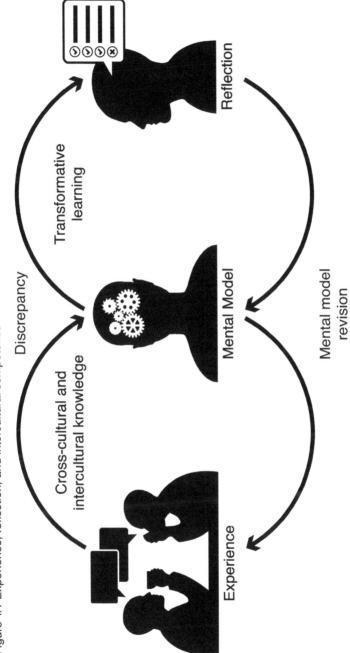

Figure 1.1 Experience, reflection, and intercultural competence

Table 1.1 Stages in intercultural development

Mental Model	Monocultural	Cross-cultural	Intercultural
Levels of understanding	Has limited understanding of cross-cultural differences or intercultural processes. Is unaware of cultural assumptions, implicit universalistic assumptions, general stereotypes about other cultures.	Uses simple explicit models of cultural influences on behavior. Has general knowledge about other cultures.	Has complex, situationally dependent models of cultural influences on behavior.
Cultural discrepancies	Relies on own culture-based mental models of interpersonal behavior. Notices symptoms of intercultural problems.	Identifies the presence of cultural discrepancies and problems.	Identifies the dynamic unfolding of interaction, is aware of demands and constraints of the situation, and is conscious of own role in shaping situation.
Solution to intercultural problems	Fixes symptoms using own cultural framework.	Adapts simple behaviors to fit the other culture.	Influences the process of the interaction to facilitate understanding.
Development Strategy	Exposure to other cultural frameworks and critical reflection toward recognizing cultural influences on self.	Development of intercultural sensemaking skills. Development of a new repertoire of thoughts and behaviors.	Continuous learning through experience and self-reflection.

knowledge and skills to deal with intercultural interactions. When facing a problem, they will attempt to fix the symptoms but may not understand the causes of the problem. For example, you ask your Chinese colleague if she agrees with your proposal and she says, "yes," but does not follow through. You assume she is unreliable and do not consider a different understanding of what "yes" means in this situation. (In China, "yes" may mean, "Yes, I hear you" as opposed to, "Yes, I agree.")

A monocultural mental model is often the result of a monocultural life experience, because of either lack of exposure to or lack of engagement with other cultures. That is, individuals may live in highly diverse neighborhoods and travel on vacation to other countries but not integrate cultural diversity into how they view life, therefore maintaining a monocultural mental model.

The first step in the development of intercultural competence is to acquire basic *cross-cultural* knowledge. Assuming openness and willingness to learn about other cultures, those of us with a monocultural mental model will benefit from cross-cultural training that emphasizes the transfer of cultural knowledge. Through exposure to basic information about several cultures, we gain awareness of ways in which people may behave differently across cultures. At this stage, it is helpful to seek the guidance of a coach or instructor to make sense of cultural differences in a way that facilitates awareness of our own cultural repertoire and helps us achieve our goals.[14]

A Cross-cultural Mental Model

Individuals with a *cross-cultural mental model* understand cultural differences through observation, study, or travel experiences. They recognize that cultures are different and influence behavior, and they may follow some simple, explicit cultural rules (e.g., do not challenge the boss in hierarchical cultures). When facing an intercultural interaction, these individuals can identify the presence of cultural discrepancies and problems (e.g., we disagree about punctuality) but may lack behavioral skills beyond adapting to fit the other culture or expecting that the other will adapt.

A cross-cultural mental model is the aggregation of many cultural schemas. Schemas are knowledge structures that store information, judgments, and feelings. The terms "schemas" and "mental models" have been used differently across disciplines, and sometimes the terms are used interchangeably. In this volume, I refer to schemas as independent knowledge structures that hold information about objects or events (e.g., desks or meetings) and mental models as more complex aggregates of schemas that include information about objects, meanings, and behaviors (meanings and feelings around meetings).

As we encounter new cultural information and have new intercultural experiences, new schemas are created but may not be assembled into a coherent intercultural mental model fitted to guide behavior in a variety of situations. For example, we may learn about meeting behaviors in different cultures but may not be able to integrate this piece of knowledge into our own understanding of meetings. This problem becomes more severe as our exposure to cultural information expands without an increase in our ability to process it.

Nowadays, cultural information is an inexpensive commodity. As a result of advances in communication and information technology, we are surrounded by cultural information. We can quickly search online for facts about any culture we may be interested in and are bombarded with information about things happening all over the world. However, our abundant information environment is fraught with contradictions, misinformation, biases, and generalizations that may not be useful or helpful in making us more competent to work across cultures. For example, you may have heard on the news that the cultural practice of touching the bodies of deceased family members in West Africa is a major challenge in controlling the spread of the Ebola epidemic.[15] If you are not a health-care worker and are not directly involved with West Africa, chances are you have no idea how to make sense of this piece of information, and it is likely that your behavior will not change because of it. Worse still, by unconsciously absorbing numerous fragments of information such as this from the media, you may develop an image of West Africa and its people that is far removed from reality and may not even be aware that you are doing so. The tradeoff we face as a result of the increased availability of information is a high level of fragmentation in how this information is made available to us, leading to challenges in making sense of this information in constructive ways. Nigerian novelist Chimamanda Adichie discussed in a TED talk her experiences of cultural misunderstanding when she moved to the United States for her education:

> My American roommate was shocked by me. She asked where I had learned to speak English so well, and was confused when I said that Nigeria happened to have English as its official language ... What struck me was this: She had felt sorry for me even before she saw me. Her default position towards me, as an African, was a kind of patronizing, well-meaning pity. My roommate had a single story of Africa: a single story of catastrophe. In this single story, there was no possibility of Africans being similar to her in any way, no possibility of feelings more complex than pity, no possibility of a connection as human equals.[16]

Individuals with a cross-cultural mental model do not necessarily need more cultural information to increase their intercultural competence. Rather, they need the ability to make sense of cultural information and to develop the skills to draw on the information that is available for more effective action. The development path from a cross-cultural to an intercultural mental model includes *critical reflection* aimed at better sensemaking skills (discussed in chapter 2). This development path relies on a willingness to suspend judgment and tolerate ambiguity and a desire to engage with cultural others for mutual benefit.

An Intercultural Mental Model

A sophisticated *intercultural mental model* is more complex than a *cross-cultural mental model* and includes *self- and situational awareness*. Individuals with high levels of intercultural competence understand that there is a potentially wide range of norms and behaviors across situations and are acutely aware of the situation unfolding in front of them. Individuals holding an intercultural mental model are not only able to identify the dynamics of an unfolding interaction, and the demands and constraints imposed on the situation by culture and other situational factors, but are also highly aware of their own role in shaping their situations. Individuals with an *intercultural mental model* are critically aware of how and why their assumptions constrain what they perceive, understand, and feel. They can use this awareness to draw on a repertoire of behaviors to influence and shape the interaction to facilitate understanding and create opportunities for cooperation.

Mental models are constantly evolving. As we become aware of our available repertoire of behaviors and experiment with different ways of selecting and combining our behavioral skills, we refine our repertoire to better meet the demands of specific intercultural situations and inform future intercultural interactions.[17] This book is written to help you move from a cross-cultural to an intercultural mental model. In other words, it will build on your understanding of the role of culture in influencing behavior to allow you to develop a more sophisticated understanding of intercultural interactions. As I discuss in chapter 2, reflection is a critical component of this process.

The Road Ahead

The cultural challenges we are likely to face in the multicultural reality of today's workplace are often messy, indeterminate, and ambiguous and do not come labeled with a simple solution. The premise of this book is that developing intercultural competence is the most viable path to equip us to mitigate the challenges and take advantage of the many benefits inherent in cultural diversity. The development of intercultural competence is a long process based on increased awareness, reflection, and experimentation.

The main goal of this book is to take you through a process of self-reflection aimed at developing your intercultural competence. This book draws on research into reflective practice and will invite you to observe, probe, analyze, and synthesize what is happening around you to enable you to better understand your role in shaping and enacting intercultural situations. Through reading this book and engaging in the suggested activities and reflections, you will develop skills to deal with ambiguous and dynamic intercultural situations, recognize your own role in shaping intercultural interactions, and identify behavioral choices suitable for each situation.

Even though the aim of this book is to help you be more successful in the workplace, you will notice that often the discussions get personal. There are two reasons for this. First, being able to think interculturally is not something that we store in our briefcase and open during work meetings. It is a way of thinking that must become second nature and be a natural part of how we approach life. Second, it is often easier to notice and understand the role of culture in ordinary life contexts than in the complex world of work. In highly multicultural and multinational work situations, we can't always clearly identify when the problems we face are a product of cultural differences, organizational characteristics, or situational factors. A focus on simpler everyday examples allows us to see the influence of culture on our thinking more clearly and to develop the skills that we will need in more complex work situations. The next chapter discusses the process of reflection in more detail.

Reflective Exercise

At the end of every chapter, a reflective exercise is proposed. The next chapter examines the logic behind these exercises and how to benefit the most from them. The exercises are aimed at helping you consider the main concepts discussed in the chapter as they relate to your own personal experience. As you work on these exercises, allow yourself the freedom to write whatever comes into your mind without much concern for grammar or doing it "right." This is writing for your own learning, and nobody is to judge it. Try to have fun!

This first exercise aims to get you started with a practice reflection in which you reflect upon your own intercultural development. For this first exercise, allow yourself fifteen minutes of uninterrupted time.

Write
For five minutes, write down as many words as you can think of to describe your past and present intercultural experiences.

Revisit
After you are done, look at your list and highlight the words that stick out as the most meaningful descriptions of your beliefs about intercultural interactions. Explore whether they are positive, negative, or both. Consider how your views of intercultural interactions came to be. Is your way of thinking based on experiences while traveling abroad, interacting with foreigners at home, or information from the media? Acknowledge your existing beliefs about intercultural interactions nonjudgmentally and allow them to evolve as you work through this book.

Prepare for the Future
Create an intercultural development plan for yourself. Consider the following questions:

- How do you assess yourself based on the stages of intercultural development presented in table 1.1?
- How do you assess your cross-cultural knowledge? Do you need to learn more about other cultures?
- Would you like to engage in this learning by yourself or would you benefit from the help of a coach or a learning buddy?

Key Points

- The ability to interact with people of other cultures is essential for success in today's workplace.

- Intercultural interactions are often ambiguous, and it is not always clear which cultural rules apply. Cross-cultural knowledge – the knowledge of how behaviors are different across cultural groups – while helpful, is insufficient.
- *Intercultural competence* is the ability to influence or shape the process of an intercultural interaction in ways that facilitate understanding. Intercultural competence focuses on the process of interaction.
- Intercultural learning requires reflection on experience to change mental models. A *mental model* is a picture in our mind of how the world works.
- *An intercultural mental model* is complex. An individual with an intercultural mental model can identify the dynamic unfolding of an interaction, is aware of the demands and constraints of the situation, and is conscious of her own role in shaping the situation.

CHAPTER 2

Building Intercultural Competence through Reflection

By three methods we may learn wisdom: First, by reflection, which is noblest; second, by imitation, which is easiest; and third, by experience, which is the bitterest.

Confucius, Chinese philosopher, 551–479 BCE

Our fast-paced work culture places a high premium on action. We are constantly on the go, bombarded with streams of fragmentary information, and compelled to keep up with massive amounts of knowledge and a large to-do list. We want fast, "how-to" answers that will help us get through our to-do list as quickly and efficiently as possible. While we may feel a sense of accomplishment when we cross items off our to-do list, our emphasis on action comes at a cost. When we emphasize action, we often neglect the meaning of information and experience and its corresponding implications for action. This shortcoming is particularly acute in many intercultural interactions we regularly face in the workplace when effective action requires *a critical reconsideration of our assumptions* accompanied by behavior that does not come to us automatically.

Consider your last working day. How much time did you spend *doing* things? How much time did you spend *thinking* about how to better approach the work you were doing? How much time did you spend *learning* from the experiences you had during the day?

Research suggests that learning and performance are enhanced when we deliberately think about what we have been doing and intentionally focus on synthesizing, abstracting, and articulating lessons learned through the experience.[1] Reflection on experience helps in many different areas of our work life but is particularly important in intercultural interactions.[2]

Intercultural interactions are highly varied. What works in one situation may not work in the next, and there are no guidebooks or answers that apply to every situation. Intercultural interactions are dynamic and ambiguous experiences that simultaneously shape and are shaped by the actions of the people involved. Think about how conversations evolve as different individuals take turns in speaking and sometimes end up in a very different place from what was initially anticipated. Everything we say, think, or do influences what the other person needs to respond to. The outcome of this process is that an interaction is highly dynamic and ambiguous. We can't mathematically add and subtract all the components to understand what has happened, why it happened, and the implications of what happened. This is where reflection comes in.

Reflection and Intercultural Competence

Reflection is a thinking process that consists of focusing our mind on *critically* examining a thought, event, or situation in an attempt to make it more comprehensible and to learn from it.[3] Reflection is an active and purposeful exploration in which we examine what we see, what happened, how we perceive a situation, how we think others perceive the same situation, and how we feel about the situation and, through this process, develop a more coherent set of ideas, or a better *story* that will inform our future actions. A *critical* examination of a situation entails challenging our own stories – questioning our assumptions, thoughts, and feelings. As such, reflection is more than just thinking about something. Reflection is an in-depth consideration of situations in an attempt to make them more comprehensible and help us find better ways to deal with them. As discussed in more detail below, the process of reflection involves describing a situation, critically revisiting it, exploring its implications for the future, and validating our newly developed theories through new actions.

Just take a moment – it does not have to be long. Think of a situation when you last interacted with someone you thought was culturally very different from you. Ask yourself, "Did I respond in the most effective way?" You might wonder what "effective" is in this situation. You might think about what has influenced your behavior. You might think about the assumptions you had going into the interaction. You might consider the details of the interaction, the words you used, the gestures you made. You might consider your feelings during and after the event. Was it a good or bad experience? Why?

These questions can lead you to explore and make sense of the experience and learn from it so you are better equipped to deal with similar situations in the future. These questions, if asked often and answered honestly, can open the door to a more interculturally competent pattern of behavior. Reflection, especially critical reflection, facilitates the identification, examination, and modification of the personal mental models that guide our behavior. As such, reflection makes us better equipped to consider alternative approaches when dealing with people from other cultures. As education scholar Richard Winter aptly said, "We do not 'store' experience as data, like a computer: we 'story' it."[4] The reflection we engage in as we craft our own stories helps us integrate a concept within our personal knowledge structures and relate that concept with things previously known,[5] adjusting our mental models to better deal with problems in the future. In short, *reflection is thinking that facilitates learning.*

Contact with new cultures challenges our understanding of who we are, how we fit into society, and how we relate to others. We may find that our habitual behaviors do not bring the desired results and that our assumptions about the world, about ourselves, or about others do not hold true. Reflection helps us make sense of situations by increasing our awareness of details we may have overlooked – of

Figure 2.1 Reflection and action

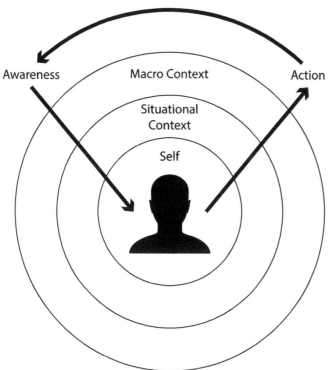

our thoughts, feelings, and taken-for-granted assumptions – opening the door to questioning them. As such, reflection makes us better equipped to consider alternative behaviors when dealing with people from other cultures. In addition, reflection helps us cope with the feelings of discomfort, anxiety, or confusion that emerge when things turn out to be different from the way we think they should be (see chapter 7). As illustrated in figure 2.1, reflection facilitates action by increasing our awareness of our situations (see chapters 3 and 6) and ourselves (see chapters 4 and 5) and through this increased awareness helps us identify appropriate courses of action.

The power of reflection lies in its ability to encourage us to stand back from what is happening and to examine our own thinking about intercultural interactions *on a regular basis*. Even though in popular speech we may sometimes use the term "reflection" loosely to mean "thinking about something," the disciplined developmental reflection we are talking about here is not a process that comes naturally to most people. Disciplined reflection is hard work and can be painful! Reflection requires challenging our assumptions, re-evaluating what we know, and letting go of our long-held, cherished beliefs and previous interpretations until new ones can be formed. It requires dealing with the ambiguity of not knowing – of not having our familiar truths to hang on to.

The Reflective Process

Reflection is a process of *dialogue* with ourselves, with the narratives we create, with our own insights, and with others as we explore the validity of our newly developed ideas and behaviors. This process is illustrated in figure 2.2 and explained below.

1. Describe Experience: Tell Your Story

The process of reflection starts by writing down your *story*. This is an opportunity to engage in self-dialogue and increase your awareness of the details of an experience or situation. In writing your story, consider where you were, who was involved, why you were there, what happened, what your role was in the situation, what others' roles were, what the results were, and how you felt about the results. Stories are a powerful way to help us make sense of experience.[6] Stories help us integrate and connect bits of experience, facts, and conjectures, organizing them into a causal order. Telling our story helps us to create order and make complex situations more manageable. When we write our story, we have the power of hindsight and can identify links and fill in information that was not available at the time the experience took place. As organizational scholar Karl Weick puts it, "Stories posit a history for an outcome. They gather strands of experience into a plot that produces an

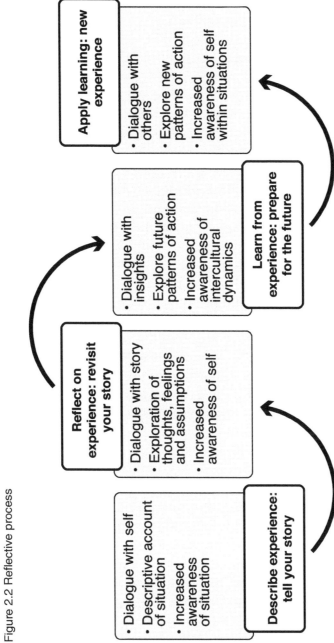

Figure 2.2 Reflective process

outcome."[7] Consider this reflection excerpt from a Venezuelan professional upon relocation to Canada: "I copied [my friend's] cover letter, adapted it to my area and on Friday I started to use the new cover letter and an improved résumé, and decided to give it 15 days to see if it worked ... My big surprise was on Monday (yes, just from Friday to Monday) when I received 3 calls for 3 different interviews!"[8] Through the ordering of events (changed cover letter, got job interview), she has developed theories about causality (changing the cover letter helped in getting a job interview). These conclusions may not necessarily be correct, but the reflective process makes them visible and accessible for further investigation.

The process of describing our story in detail helps us become more aware of our context – of our taken-for-granted assumptions and practices – and gain control over our actions. For instance, when entering a new intercultural situation, such as joining a new organization or community or moving to another country, we are faced with a new cultural context and need to consider which aspects of the new culture we will appropriate, how we will adapt to the new circumstances, and which aspects of the situation we can modify to fit our own interests. By exploring a situation in detail, focusing on aspects we might have thought were irrelevant, we become more attuned to small changes that can make a difference. For example, we may notice a subtle change in behavior by one of the individuals involved in the interaction that can have important implications that we may have overlooked. Through reflection we think through a situation and gain a better understanding of what happened, how we played a role in what happened, and what we can do about it. (See chapter 3 for more on how situational awareness plays a key role in the development of intercultural competence.)

When reflecting, we do not need extraordinary stories. Ordinary everyday situations that at first may look inconsequential may provide a better ground for developmental reflection because we are more open to look at them. Challenging situations create anxiety, which we are motivated to resolve. When reflecting, we may try to soothe our anxiety by using defense mechanisms (of course

I am right and she is wrong). In these cases, our reflections can help us feel better but not help us learn.[9] On the other hand, when reflecting on seemingly unproblematic situations, we may find that we are more receptive and willing to question our assumptions and behaviors.

2. Reflect on Experience: Revisit Your Story

The power of stories lies in their ability to compress and frame a large number of thoughts, events, and facts into a simple, ordered sequence of events. However, stories conceal the assumptions and beliefs that led to these connections. When we reflect, we order pieces of information into coherent stories. We order things chronologically and we assign causality based on premises we hold. Those premises are things we know to be facts, things we believe, things we assume based on cultural or personal knowledge. For example, suppose you met Mary in the hallway and she rushed past you with a "See you later." You may hold views about appropriate behavior in casual encounters based on your beliefs about relationships, your cultural knowledge about norms of behavior (e.g., ask about personal well-being when meeting acquaintances), or your knowledge of Mary (e.g., Mary is always friendly). You may start with your observations about what you noticed about Mary (she rushed past me). You order those facts chronologically (we had a disagreement yesterday, and she rushed past me today). You then start to work on explanations. You may come up with a story like this: Mary was upset with me and did not stop to talk. This comes from reasoning: *People stop to chat when things are well. Mary did not stop to talk. Therefore, she must be upset. Therefore, she rushed past me because she is upset.*

It is a principle of good reasoning that if your premises are wrong, your conclusions are also wrong.[10] Thus, having good premises or good assumptions is critical. In a monocultural situation, this means having more and better information about people and their situations. In an intercultural situation, the task of knowing what is happening can get a bit more complicated, because while we need to evaluate the validity of our premises, we may not have a good way to do that. There are always many alternative explanations for the behavior we are observing, and it may be difficult to identify the most plausible one. A very risky alternative is to replace the premises based on cultural stereotypes. A better alternative would be to further investigate to gain information that helps us understand what is happening. But before we do that, we need to *know what we don't know.*

Reflection helps us to become aware of the assumptions we are making and opens the door to questioning them. When we "story" a situation in our minds, we order and connect facts, observations, and assumptions, unconsciously filling in the gaps in our knowledge. We rely on our previous knowledge and interpretation schemas to make sense of new situations. In intercultural situations, these interpretation schemas and this previous knowledge may be inappropriate and need to be revised. Reflection helps us notice how we are using our assumptions, helps us identify the limits of our knowledge, and guides us into seeking more information. By helping us to revisit our assumptions, reflection encourages us to adopt new perspectives, which can help us come up with new solutions to problems and identify new behavioral alternatives.

Sue, a marketing professional, offered the following reflection on her interactions in a recent networking event: "I realized that … talking to anyone that I feel inferior to ramps up my anxieties … I feel as though I am bothering them or have nothing to offer to the conversation. This of course is not true … when I reflected upon [a specific situation] and how the other person communicated with me, I felt that it was my own projection, and in reality, the other person was not communicating that at all. My insecurities … caused me to perceive the situation differently than it was actually occurring at the time." Sue came out of her interaction feeling that she did not have anything to offer to the conversation. When she took the time to reflect upon the details of the situation, she realized that her interpretation of the situation was clouded by her own insecurities.

A careful consideration of the behavior of the people involved helped her see her own role in shaping her experience.

After you are done writing your story, pause and read what you have written with an open and curious mind. Ask yourself, "What is significant in what I have written with regard to becoming more interculturally competent?" "What might I do differently in the future?"

As you consider your story, you might ask the following questions:

- Are there facts, thoughts, or details not considered in my story that could change the interpretation of the story?
- How was I feeling, and why did I feel that way?
- What assumptions were guiding my actions?
- What knowledge might have influenced me?
- What was I trying to achieve, and I did I respond effectively?
- What were others' feelings, and why did they feel that way?
- What were the consequences of my actions for others and myself?
- How does this situation connect with other experiences?
- How might I reframe this situation to respond more effectively?
- What might have been the consequences if I had responded differently?
- What factors might prevent me from responding in new ways?
- How do I feel NOW about this experience?
- What insights have I gained? What did I learn from this experience?

Revisiting your story is a powerful way to understand the leaps and assumptions you made in constructing your story, to challenge your assumptions, and to question the connections made that are conjectural and perhaps incorrect. If you enjoy the story-telling approach, you might attempt to write the story from the other person's point of view and compare differences in sequencing, causality, or interpretations (e.g., write the story as if you were your boss rather than yourself). You might also consider writing the continuation of that story. What did the other person do after your interaction? You might write a fictional story in which the person goes home and discusses the event with his or her family. What would the person have said? You might also consider changing facts or behaviors and play with alternative plots. What might happen if ...? The important thing at this stage is to critically assess the validity of your story and its usefulness in guiding your behavior. When revisiting your story and reflecting on a situation, it is important to go beyond *what* happened and what the results were to try to uncover *why* things happened.

3. Learn from Experience: Prepare for the Future

The process of writing and reflecting upon your behavior helps you understand what happened, but the biggest benefit is in using this understanding to guide future actions. After you have reflected on an event and pondered the root causes of the behaviors and outcomes of that situation, it is important for you to consider the implications of this insight for the future.

Reflection helps us update our mental models and develop new theories of action. Through reflection, we continuously take stock of our experiences, reorganize them, and construct new models or understandings. By reconstructing our experiences, we are able to edit some details out, bring other details in, and through this process reorganize our thoughts and construct more accurate mental models that will help us deal with similar situations in the future. Consider this reflection about French and Canadians written by a French blogger living in Canada: "eventually I developed a theory: French people are not rude, they just defend their territory and tend to be distrustful at times. However, they are extremely friendly and generous with those close to them, such as family and friends. On the other hand, Canadians tend to be polite and treat strangers better. But they value their privacy and personal space and are more reserved, even around their friends and relatives ... and all that can be interpreted as rudeness by foreigners!"[11] Through reflection she was able to develop a new understanding about French and Canadian approaches to relationships and mutual perceptions of rudeness. Her new theory may not necessarily be "right" or complete, but once it has been articulated it can be validated either through dialogue with Canadians or through further experimentation and observation (see step 4 below).

At this point we need to ask, "So what?" and "Now what?" In other words, we need to consider the implications of our discoveries and identify the actions that need to be taken in the future. This may mean needing to go back to that individual or situation and say things that were left unsaid. Perhaps it means we need to approach interactions in different ways. We may identify skills we need to develop, or gaps in our knowledge we need to bridge. Perhaps we realize that there are things we do not know about a situation that we need to find out before we can fully understand what is happening.

Sometimes there may be nothing that can be done about an interaction. In that case, you need to consider its implications for future situations. Should you do something differently in the future? Can you transfer this learning to other contexts? Is there something you need to learn more about? Is there something you discovered about yourself that will help you in the future?

4. Apply Learning: New Experiences

Reflection can help us develop skills for intercultural interaction. When we make sense of an intercultural situation through reflection, we *need to validate our conclusions* by testing them out or by engaging in dialogue with others who may challenge our interpretations and help us identify alternative explanations and points of view. The reflective cycle is thus only completed when we go back into the world and apply what we have learned to improve our interactions. Action at this stage may mean engaging in dialogue with others to deepen our insights, gather additional information, or check our understanding. It may also mean changing our habitual behaviors and engaging in new patterns of action. This step is critical in continuous learning, as there is no guarantee that the process of reflection will lead to good or correct conclusions. It is only when the newly developed theories are tested out in the world that the reflective process is completed.

The process of reflection will – most of the time – change the way we think about a situation. Reflection allows us to reconsider our assumptions, develop new theories, and identify new avenues of behavior. However, there is no guarantee that our new conclusion is "right" or "good." Reflection is only the first step in the process of learning more about ourselves, about the role of culture, and about the others with whom we are interacting. Reflection must be supported by continuous engagement with others and a commitment to continuous learning.

Making the Most of Reflections

Developing a habit of reflection may be challenging. As was discussed earlier, we tend to favor action over thinking. We may also feel that we are not getting enough out of the time and effort devoted to reflection. Below I offer some suggestions to make the most of a reflective practice.

1. Prepare for Reflection

To get the most out of our reflection process, we need to create the time, space, and mental clarity required for it. Choose a comfortable place and time where you are not likely to be interrupted. *Free writing* is a good way to prepare for reflection.[12] Give yourself a few minutes to write freely without concern about what you are writing. Do not worry about coherence, spelling, or grammar. Just write down whatever comes to your mind without judgment. If your mind jumps between thoughts, let it jump. For five minutes, just follow your mind. You may write about your day, about your feelings, remember you forgot to buy tomatoes, remember you need to do the laundry, and then return to your feelings. This is not your reflection, this is a time to clear your mind and prepare for your reflection. Writer and creative coach Julia Cameron suggests people interested in being more creative should do this type of free writing every morning to clear the mind and open space for more creative thoughts to emerge.[13] This type of mind-clearing writing is especially important before a reflection exercise in which your goal is to question your own thinking. After you have finished your five minutes of free writing, put it aside. You do not need to come back to it.

2. Write It Down

You may be wondering, "Why bother writing?" when you can just as easily think about your intercultural experiences in your head. Writing and other types of visual language such as images, shapes, doodles, and conceptual maps facilitate thinking and learning in several ways. First, putting things down on paper (or on a screen) extends our mind and increases our ability to work with complex issues. Cognitive science tells us that the typical human brain can only keep a very small amount of information in working memory at any given point in time. As a result, instead of keeping all the relevant details about a situation in our minds, we physically store and manipulate those details out in the world, in the very situation itself.[14] Think about counting using your fingers as support, or writing down directions to a new location as opposed to memorizing them. Our fingers and paper act as extensions of our mind, releasing cognitive power to focus on other things, as we know that the information will not be lost. When we put thoughts down on paper through writing or drawing, we allow our minds to release that information from our short-term memory and free cognitive power to organize, examine, and reflect on its deeper implications.

Putting things down on paper through writing, drawing, doodling, or mapping helps us achieve coherence by organizing, clarifying, and sequencing our thoughts. When we are thinking in our head, we are free to change topics, drop lines of reasoning, get distracted with something else, and often get stuck in a loop, returning to the same thought repeatedly. For example, we may think that what the other person said or did was rude and keep going over all the details of the event that support our thoughts and feelings.

When we record our experience, we can step back, look at it, know how we understand it, and challenge our own thinking.

The process of writing also helps us to develop a reflective habit and witness our growth over time. We are more likely to remain focused on a task if we have a time assigned for it. In addition, the very process of moving the pen across the paper (or typing on a keyboard) anchors us in the present moment and prevents our thoughts from wandering.[15] Writing also captures thoughts for later consideration. As we continue with this process day after day, we are able to notice patterns over time and track our progress. As we reflect, we may have an insight or thought that, if not written down, will be forgotten. As we revisit our notes, we can capture and revisit those insights. By recording our thoughts, we are able to provide ourselves with feedback, relate to past and future, and respond to our own thinking.

3. Enlist Help

The process of reflection is not always pleasant and may be easier if facilitated by a coach, mentor, or reflection partner.[16] While writing reflective journals is private and focused primarily on self-discovery, sharing personal reflections with a mentor or coach or exposing selective thoughts to others who may provide critical insight has the potential to accelerate the development of intercultural competence. When possible, it is helpful to engage a reflection buddy – someone who is willing to work with you on this process and challenge you to see things in different ways, someone whose job is not to agree with you but to help you see things from a different perspective and challenge your assumptions.

4. Give It Time

The process of reflecting on experiences is a powerful tool to promote learning and growth. But that does not mean that every time we reflect we gain big insights. The process of moving toward new understanding and the construction of new mental models is not linear and predictable. The outcomes may not be immediate, but they will come. And that is why it is important to think about reflective journaling as a *practice*, or a regular and consistent activity.

Becoming Reflective

While reflection is critical to the development of intercultural competence, an interculturally competent person can reflect *in* action as well as reflect *on* action that has already passed. The ability to reflect *in* action has been referred to as *mindfulness*[17] or *reflexivity*[18] and is considered a central element in facilitating intercultural and interpersonal interactions. Education scholar Christopher Johns,[19] an expert on reflective practice, suggests a typology of reflective practice ranging from merely doing reflection (reflecting on past actions) to being reflective (seeing things as they are within the moment). In his typology, reflection-in-action is an intermediate stage in which we can stand back in the middle of action and redirect our actions toward a desired outcome.

The quality of being reflective, or mindfulness, is characterized by a constant awareness of the following:

1. our own attitudes, assumptions, thoughts, and actions
2. the other person's attitudes, assumptions, words, and behaviors
3. the context of the interaction and changes in the context
4. our own roles in shaping the context of the interaction and influencing the behavior of others
5. our emotions and how they may be influencing our ability to act appropriately

Becoming reflective requires the development of a reflective habit. When reflecting-*on*-action becomes second nature, the insights and thinking processes become available to use during interactions and allow us to learn on the fly,[20] responding appropriately to situations as they develop.

The Road Ahead

Intercultural learning is a process that involves feelings, relationships with others, and subconscious ways of knowing. Intercultural learning involves a reassessment of who we are, which happens by reflecting with a curious mind on our thoughts and feelings during our everyday interactions, probing the implications of our habits of mind for the way we behave. Developing intercultural competence is a long-term process. While you are reading this book – and for as long afterwards as possible – bring your awareness to your behavior in intercultural situations and reflect upon their implications. Analyze, probe, investigate, and be curious in an effort to understand yourself. The next chapter introduces a process of reflecting on the situated nature of our interactions.

Reflective Exercise

This first formal reflective exercise aims to help you gain some experience with the reflective approach proposed in this chapter and to give you the opportunity to explore how you typically approach intercultural experiences. This is your basic reflection, which will be used as a starting point in the following chapters. As you select situations for reflection, remember that they do not need to be dramatic. They could be ordinary, everyday situations that you perhaps felt did not deserve much of your attention. The reflective exercise proposes several questions for consideration. Start by writing your story in a way that makes sense to you, and then, after you are done, reread the questions and add details you may have missed.

Tell Your Story (Step 1)
Write a detailed description of an intercultural situation. Draw on all your senses and make your description as rich and detailed as possible. What was the context of this situation? Who was there? What was influencing your behavior? What did you say or do? What did others say or do? How were you feeling?

Revisit Your Story (Step 2)

Leave your story aside for at least one hour. Then revisit your story by asking yourself the following questions:

- Are there facts, thoughts, or details not considered in your description that could change your interpretation of the story?
- What assumptions were guiding your actions? What knowledge might have influenced you?
- When interacting with others, what were you trying to achieve? Did you respond effectively? What were the consequences of your actions for others and yourself? What would be the consequences had you responded differently? What factors might prevent you from responding in new ways?
- How did you feel and why did you feel that way? How did your feelings influence your actions? What were others' feelings and why did they feel that way? How do you feel about this experience now?
- How does this situation connect with other experiences?

Prepare for the Future and Apply Learning (Steps 3 and 4)

- What insights have you gained from this experience, and what are their implications for the future?
- Does this situation require further action? Of what kind? Are there things you need to say or do? Are there knowledge gaps you need to cover? How can you validate your conclusions?
- Based on what you have learned, how are you approaching new situations?

Key Points

- *Reflection* is a thinking process that consists of focusing our mind on critically examining a thought, event, or situation in an attempt to make it more comprehensible and to learn from it.
- *Reflection* is a process of *dialogue* with ourselves, with the narratives we create, with our own insights, and with others as we explore the validity of our newly developed ideas and behaviors.

- The reflective process consists of four steps: 1) tell your story – describe the experience; 2) revisit your story – reflect on your experience; 3) prepare for the future – learn from experience; 4) engage in new experience – apply learning.
- To make the most of reflection it is important to prepare for reflection, creating the time, space, and mental clarity for it. It also helps to write down reflections, enlist help, and give it time.
- Intercultural competence requires becoming reflective, which involves being aware of an unfolding situation as we are immersed in it, including the following: our own and others' attitudes, assumptions, and behaviors; the context of the interaction; our own role in shaping the interaction; and the role of our emotions in shaping our behavior.

CHAPTER 3

Situating Intercultural Interactions

Toto, I've got a feeling we're not in Kansas anymore.

Dorothy in *The Wizard of Oz*

We do not live in a vacuum. We live in a world made up of people, places, things, and activities that shape how we think and act. We move from one situation to the next and often change our thinking and behavior as our context changes. We may be calm and relaxed at the yoga studio and shift into a hurried and stressed mode as soon as we arrive at the office. We may be confident and articulate at work but feel insecure and self-conscious at a dance class. We may be a top performer at headquarters but flounder abroad. Our surroundings matter and influence our mood, perceptions, attitudes, and behaviors. Our surrounding circumstances influence what becomes salient or important, how we interpret things, and which behaviors are appropriate. As radio host Terry O'Reilly wittily said, "There is definitely nothing wrong with kicking back in your underwear, putting your feet up on the furniture and scarfing back a cold beer ... unless you are interviewing to a position of CFO for a multinational software giant."[1] Context has an important role in defining what behavior is appropriate or inappropriate in everyday life.

I am writing this chapter at the cottage, on a cool early morning in August. I got up before everybody else, turned on the coffee maker, and am sitting by the window looking at a lake covered in fog. I hear the silence of nature. I feel relaxed and energized and find it easy to write. The troubles and distractions of my everyday life have stayed behind in the city. In pajamas, amid nature, I feel less constrained by the demands and expectations of the academic community. I think differently; I behave differently; I write differently.

Consider your present circumstances. Where are you right now? Is it a pleasant or unpleasant location? How much time do you have? Who is around you? How are your current circumstances influencing the way you feel, think, or behave?

The role of context in shaping behavior has important implications for intercultural interactions. As I discuss in more detail in the next chapter, cultural influences on behavior vary by context. As we approach diverse intercultural situations in the course of our work, we need to become aware of how our context is influencing our behaviors and the dynamics of our intercultural interactions, as well as how our behaviors are influencing the context for others involved. The main goal of this chapter is to call attention to the interrelationship between context and behavior. The next chapters delve more deeply into how culture and context matter and what we can do to make positive changes to our circumstances.

Putting Things in Context:
Situating Intercultural Interactions

Intercultural interactions are exchanges between individuals from different cultures *within a context*. Consider how the following situations may be different:

• You are purchasing a souvenir from a Moroccan salesperson in the *suq* in Marrakech during your holiday.

Figure 3.1 Intercultural interactions

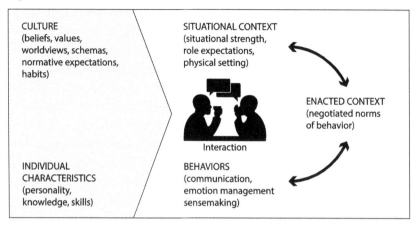

- You are negotiating a deal between your organization and a Moroccan organization for a long-term purchase agreement in your office in New York.
- You are collaborating on a research project with a Moroccan co-worker during a conference meeting in Paris.

Even though these three situations have the same national cultures involved, they are very different, presenting different cultural challenges and requiring different thoughts and behaviors. In the first case, you might do well by just reminding yourself you are in Marrakech and following the old adage, "When in Rome, do as the Romans do," while in the third case, being in Paris does not necessarily help you much in identifying the best behavior.

Intercultural interactions are influenced by three major components: individual differences in preferences, values, beliefs and skills; contextual demands and constraints; and intentional behavior, or the choices we make regarding how to deal with our intercultural situations. Figure 3.1 summarizes the intercultural interaction process presented in this chapter and discussed in detail in the following chapters. *Culture* provides individuals with preferences and skills that will influence the resources they have available to deal with an intercultural situation (chapter 4). However, *individual characteristics* influence the extent to which individuals in an interaction adopt perspectives typical of their culture and are able to use knowledge and skills to go beyond their cultural boundaries (chapter 5). The *situational context* makes cultural schemas and norms salient and creates constraints and demands influencing which behaviors are possible and how individuals interact (chapter 6). The *enacted context* is the outcome of the interaction, which becomes part of the experience (chapters 3 and 6), and is dependent on individuals' *behaviors,* which may or may not facilitate understanding (chapters 7 and 8).

As depicted in figure 3.1, intercultural interactions are dynamic. Our behaviors create the situations that we need to respond to. A cultural script of what to do when facing someone from another culture is of limited help because, as we start interacting, the situation changes in unpredictable ways. This is not unique to intercultural interactions, however. We adapt our behavior, including what we think, feel, and do, as we navigate new situations in the course of a day.[2] Psychologists equate interacting with the world with white-water canoeing. A detailed script in advance is insufficient to get us safely to our destination. Rather, we must continuously make adjustments in the canoe's position as unexpected waves and currents rock our boat. While we may have preconceived ideas about how to interact with the boat, our mind needs to transform incoming information into what to do *right now*.[3] We refer to this process of continuous adjustment in the course of an intercultural interaction as *intercultural sensemaking*.

Intercultural Sensemaking

Intercultural sensemaking is the process by which individuals interacting within a social and physical context arrive at an understanding of what is going on, act based on this understanding, and by doing so further *enact*, or create, their situation.[4] Interactions with people from foreign cultures are often a catalyst for sensemaking because we must cope with the uncertainty, ambiguity, and anxiety caused by different cultural frameworks.[5] When we face a situation that does not meet our cultural expectations, we are faced with a *discrepancy* or perhaps a *surprise* that triggers a process of sensemaking.

Sensemaking organizes our understanding of cause and effect and sequencing, and as a result informs our next action or non-action. Through sensemaking, we construct an interpretation of why things turned out differently from what we expected and what we need to do as a result.[6] We engage in sensemaking processes naturally and instinctively any time we face a situation we do not understand, but our natural sensemaking process may or may not lead to better intercultural interactions. For example, if we make sense of a situation in which there are important cultural assumptions at play by concluding that the other person is crazy, uneducated, or unreliable, we are likely to behave in ways that are derogatory and create an unpleasant interaction. On the other hand, if we conclude that there are things we do not know and start asking questions respectfully, the interaction may evolve in more positive ways.

The process of intercultural sensemaking is illustrated in figure 3.2 and briefly explained below. Subsequent chapters revisit this process to delve deeper into each of these components.

The process of intercultural sensemaking depicted in figure 3.2 involves continuously interacting in a social and physical context to arrive at an understanding of what is going on. This process is cyclical and happens through communication with others as we focus attention on a set of words, body language, facial expressions, and surrounding circumstances and interpret these disparate bits of information by constructing a story of what is happening.[7] As we experience a behavior that is different from what we expect, we try to make sense of it by constructing a story that will tell us what is happening and why it is happening. Our story or interpretation will inform us how we are supposed to feel about it, and what would be the most logical next step.

For example, imagine that you come from a culture that values direct and straightforward communication. As you engage in a

Figure 3.2 Intercultural sensemaking

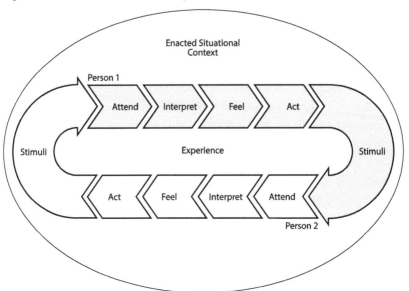

conversation with another person, you are likely to think that direct questioning is the most reasonable way to get a straightforward answer. Now assume that the individual with whom you are communicating comes from a culture that values indirect communication and the avoidance of public embarrassment. For this person, direct questions are inappropriate, and information is exchanged indirectly through subtle suggestions and hints. A likely result of this hypothetical exchange is that you will ask a direct question and will get an indirect answer, which you may perceive to be an unsatisfactory response. At this point you will experience a discrepancy that requires sensemaking: "What is going on here?" and "What should I do?"

Based on your observation of the situation or on things that caught your attention, you will attempt to come up with a theory or interpretation to explain what is going on. It may be that you noticed that the other person had an accent and perhaps interpreted the problem as "she did not understand my question," or you noticed some embarrassment and concluded that "she did not appreciate my question." Depending on your interpretation of the problem, you may experience different feelings, which could be frustration, compassion, or curiosity. As a result, you may engage in a new action such as repeating the question, rephrasing the question, or dropping the topic altogether. Whatever you do, you will provide a stimulus for a new cycle of sensemaking as your counterpart also attempts to figure out "What is going on here?" and "What should I do?" This process is ongoing, and the interaction continues as we gather more information, craft new interpretations, and reconstruct the story of what is happening. You may start by concluding that language was a problem, discover that there are no language issues, and make a new "sense" of the situation in which some cultural differences become more salient. Furthermore, through interaction, you and your counterpart will establish new patterns of behavior, and together shape your experience.

The conclusion here is that, in an interaction, we are faced with not one objective situation but with many possible situations, which are linked to how we interpret what is going on around us. A more sophisticated understanding is that situations are created – or enacted – *through* interactions.[8] *Enactment* refers to the notion that people contribute to the construction of the situations they face through their attention and interpretation processes.[9] In other words, even though parts of our external environment exist independent of our thinking (i.e., there are objects with material properties in the environment that are independent of us), our situation is enacted through our attention, interpretation, and interactions with others. Organization scholar Barbara Czarniawska explains the relationship between people's cognition and the external environment as follows: "A stone exists independently of our cognition; but we enact it by cognitive bracketing, by concentrating our attention on it. Thus 'called to life,' or to attention, the stone must be socially constructed with the help of the concept of stone, its properties, and uses."[10]

In other words, once we focus our attention on something, it becomes an important part of our experienced context. We then label it, categorize it, and interpret it. Once we label the object in front of us as a "stone," we call to mind properties we associate with stones and rules of behavior related to stones, thus changing the way we think about our context. By interpreting the object as a stone as opposed to a sacred artifact or a weapon, we call into action a different set of behaviors to associate with that object. For example, upon entering a room we see objects with some specific material characteristics and define them individually as chairs and a table, and collectively as a "meeting room." The objects with their physical properties are independent of our thinking, but the definition of this context as a meeting room as opposed to a lunchroom happens in our mind. We then act based on our interpretations and by doing so further shape the context around us, influencing subsequent interpretations and interactions. For instance, if you interpret the room with a table and chairs as a lunchroom and start eating your lunch, the next person observing the room will notice food, further defining the space as an eating space. To take this further, the conversation the newcomer may enter into with you may be informal and more suitable to a lunchroom than to a boardroom. However, the initial objective components of the context remain unchanged – a table with chairs around it.

To go further, the notion of table and chairs relies on our cultural knowledge of what a table is supposed to look like and the uses it is supposed to have. A hypothetical individual never exposed to tables may interpret the object as a bed, a piece of art, or a weapon. We rely on our cultural and individual knowledge to label objects and experiences in ways that make sense to us. Thus, our context is not "objective" but constructed through our interactions with material and social elements present in that context. Likewise, when we interact with others, the aspects of our interaction that we focus on will influence what becomes important, how we interpret our situation, and the behaviors we think are appropriate.

Situations are dynamic and ambiguous, simultaneously shaping and being shaped by the actions of the people involved, including our own. As we notice and interpret parts of what is happening and act based on those interpretations, we create the constraints and opportunities we face. However, these constraints and opportunities do not need to be left to chance. We may play a more conscious role in shaping the interactions and situations we face through *situational awareness*.

Situational Awareness: Thinking and Acting in Context

Intercultural competence manifests itself in our ability to influence or shape an intercultural interaction so as to facilitate understanding and create opportunities for cooperation. To influence or shape an interaction, we need to be aware of the evolving situation, of our own role, and of the roles of others in shaping the situation, and to understand what can and can't be done. In other words, we need to develop *situational awareness* or the ability to consider the dynamically evolving context of an interaction while we are immersed in it.

The notion of situational awareness was first introduced in the study of pilots' performance. To make safe decisions, pilots need to be acutely aware of all elements in their environment – the wind speed and direction, the physical topography, the altitude, other planes, airspace restrictions, and so on. The pilot must be able to comprehend and project the behavior of these elements in the near future.[11] Intercultural interactions require the same type of awareness, even if the outcome of a poor intercultural decision may not be as dramatic as that of a poor piloting decision. Situational awareness is the consciousness of how contextual elements of a situation are influencing the thoughts, feelings, and behaviors of the people involved and of how people's actions further influence or modify the context of the interaction. Situational awareness provides individuals with the knowledge to generate behaviors that shape their situational context in ways that facilitate understanding and cooperation.

Chapter 1 discussed the importance of mental models, the mental pictures we hold about how the world works and how we should behave in different situations. Our mental models are instrumental in filtering the large flow of information to which we are exposed, helping us select and interpret what is important and guiding us toward action. Research on cognition suggests that our thinking is situated, that is, that the characteristics of the situation influence this filtering and interpreting process and thus influence what we do.[12] For example, psychology scholar Robert Cialdini and his colleagues conducted a series of experiments in which people had an opportunity to litter in a public space.[13] They manipulated the characteristics of the context by varying the amount of visible litter and found that people's littering behavior was influenced by how much litter they saw. People were less likely to litter when the space was clean than when it was dirty, even if they saw other people littering. They found that people would infer a *norm* of not littering when the place was clean and a norm of littering when the place was dirty and would often comply with this assumed norm. As will be discussed in the next chapter, norms are a powerful influence on our behavior and an important aspect of culture.

Other research suggests that individuals tend to unconsciously conform to the behaviors of others. Psychology scholars Tanya Chartrand and John Bargh found that individuals paired with a partner who constantly shook his foot or rubbed his head unconsciously mirrored that behavior, suggesting that some of our behaviors are reactions to external stimuli.[14] These studies suggest that context is not just a background for our actions but an important influence on what we think, feel, and do. Fashion is a good example.[15] We adjust our sense of what is acceptable or desirable in terms of hairstyle or clothing based on what we see around us, and our tastes and preferences change over time as our context changes (if you are not convinced, look at how you were dressed in your old pictures).

Context influences thinking and action in three ways: first, it focuses individuals' *attention* toward certain things and away from others. Second, it provides a system of meaning to *interpret* what is going on. Third, it limits the availability of behavioral options, thus influencing *action*. We discuss each of these in turn.

Context influences attention. Our attention is triggered by characteristics of the situation, as in the littering example above. The characteristics of a situation make some issues more salient than others and guide what we focus on. For example, if our interaction is happening in Chinatown we are more likely to notice Chinese cultural symbols and be more sensitive to the Chinese culture than if our meeting were in another part of town.[16]

Context influences interpretation. The context in which an encounter takes place provides individuals with a system of meaning with which to interpret information and behavior. People don't make sense of behaviors in a vacuum; instead, they put them in context to assign meaning to them. For example, regardless of her cultural background, a woman's decision to wear a headscarf for a meeting will be interpreted differently if she is in Tehran where headscarves are mandatory, or in Paris where headscarves are banned in some places, or in Toronto where wearing headscarves is an individual choice.

Context influences action. The characteristics of a context can influence the availability and attractiveness of behavioral options by defining the degree to which noncompliance with rules and norms is tolerated, as well as the consequences of noncompliance. These constraints may be part of the legal and cultural framework of the nation where business takes place, part of the organization's formal and informal norms, or part of the specific situation. For example, women are expected to wear a headscarf when visiting a mosque. In some contexts, this rule is strictly enforced, but in others, deviations are tolerated, even if not appreciated, such as in highly touristic secular locations.

As you read this book, think about how your attention, interpretations, and actions are being influenced by the situation in which you are reading it. Perhaps you are focusing on specific aspects of the text to fulfill the requirements of an assignment, or you are not paying much attention at all as you are concerned that you may miss your flight. You may be writing notes on the side of the page or not. Consider how the situation in which you are reading this book is shaping your reading behavior.

Layers of Context

The context of an intercultural interaction has multiple layers (see figure 3.3). At the core, there is the situational context or the immediate circumstances surrounding the interaction. The situational context is often embedded within an organizational context (e.g., IBM), a macro cultural and institutional context (e.g., Germany), and a macro historical-political context. Each one of these layers of context has a specific influence on the nature and dynamics of our interactions.

Figure 3.3 Layers of context

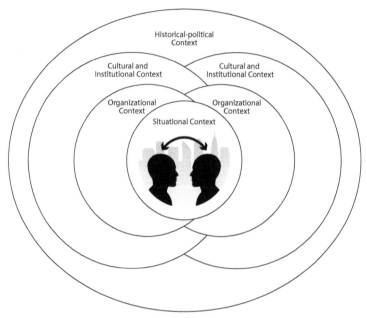

The macro *historical-political context* incorporates the global political climate that extends beyond the countries involved and may place additional pressures on individuals and exacerbate cultural differences. For example, throughout history, the perceived status of different cultural groups and the consequent regard and respect for their organizations and individuals have oscillated. The global political climate may influence business relationships subjectively by reinforcing negative stereotypes and promoting lack of trust. Objectively, individuals may fear that the overall climate will eventually result in regulations or social movements that may undermine the future of a deal or relationship.

The *cultural and institutional context* incorporates much of the macro environment in which we find ourselves. At this level, we are influenced by macro cultural influences as well as other pressures such as legal and administrative requirements. On some occasions, the institutional environment is a country, but some regional, industrial, or professional characteristics may operate across countries (e.g., European Union regulations or product standards), or be specific to regions within one country (e.g., languages and cultural norms in Wallonia, Flanders, or Brussels can vary significantly, even though these regions are all part of Belgium). In short, whether our meeting is in Venezuela, Greece, or Japan may have important implications for our behavior and interactions.

The *organizational context* incorporates the specific group or organization in which the interaction is taking place. That could be a common employer, a professional association, or any group that provides individuals with a set of rules, policies, guidelines, procedures, and norms of behavior to guide action. For example, when participating in professional international conferences, participants know how to behave regardless of where the meeting takes place. Organizational cultures may either replicate or reject national cultural values and norms, creating a microenvironment in which national norms are either reinforced or do not apply. Many global organizations deal with the challenges posed by multiple national cultures by creating clear behavioral guidelines across the organization. For example, several years ago, General Electric (GE) acquired several companies in western Europe, including Spain, Germany, France, and Italy.[17] GE's approach was to integrate these companies by imposing American management practices and culture. Among other things, managers were told that titles didn't matter and that employees would be valued based on knowledge and performance rather than their positions. In these subsidiaries, the organizational culture played an important role in shaping people's interactions by defining how people should address each other.

The *situational context* in which we find ourselves consists of the circumstances in which a specific interaction is taking place and that provide us with cues as to how to behave. The situational context is embedded in an institutional and organizational environment, but it has its own unique characteristics that will influence how an interaction evolves and how the other layers are interpreted. For instance, consider how context influences our perceptions of other cultures.

With a partner in Portugal, I conducted a study with Portuguese managers inquiring about their perceptions regarding business partners of other cultures. We found that Portuguese managers perceived business activities with Brazilians and Spaniards, with whom they are culturally more similar, to be riskier and more difficult than those with Scandinavians, who are culturally very different. However, the same managers felt more "at home" and preferred to socialize and make friends with Brazilians and Spaniards.[18] What this suggests is that cultural differences are not inherently good or bad but can be perceived positively or negatively depending on the situation in which we interact with the other culture. As is discussed in more detail in chapter 6, characteristics of the situational context may override individual and cultural preferences and cue in specific behaviors that may facilitate or hinder intercultural interactions.

I have described each layer of context separately and independently; in reality, however, different layers and aspects of context coexist and interact. That is, being on the factory floor of your organization in China or in Germany is important, and multiple layers of context act together to define the experience. Further, at different points in time, different aspects of context may be more or less dominant in influencing behavior.

The Road Ahead

Intercultural interactions are dynamic and evolve through a process of intercultural sensemaking. This sensemaking process has some important characteristics. First, it does not happen in a vacuum but within several layers of context that shape what becomes salient, how we interpret things, and the behaviors that are most appropriate. Second, individuals bring with them their own cultural resources, skills, experiences, and identities, which influence what they notice, how they interpret what they notice, how they feel about situations, and the actions they are able to undertake. Third, the process of sensemaking is *enactive*, or constructive, and is created through interactions.

Awareness of the dynamic flow of intercultural interactions is critical to improving intercultural interactions. The next chapter considers the influence of culture on behavior and intercultural interactions.

Reflective Exercise

This exercise will help you become more aware of the circumstances surrounding a situation and your role in shaping the situation.

Tell Your Story
Write a detailed description of an intercultural situation. Draw on all your senses and make your description as rich and detailed as possible. What was the context of this situation? Who was there? What was influencing your behavior? What did you say or do? What did others say or do? How were you feeling?

   In particular, consider the context of your interaction: Where were you? What were the macro cultural and institutional contexts influencing the situation? What were the organizational contexts involved for each of you? What role was each person playing? Who else may have influenced this interaction?

Revisit Your Story
Leave your story aside for at least one hour. Then, revisit your story by asking yourself the following questions:

✓ Are there facts, thoughts, or details not considered in your description that could change your interpretation of the story?
✓ What assumptions were guiding your actions? What knowledge might have influenced you?
✓ When interacting with others, what were you trying to achieve? Did you respond effectively? What were the consequences of your actions for others and yourself? What would be the consequences had you responded differently? What factors might prevent you from responding in new ways?

✓ How did you feel and why did you feel that way? How did your feelings influence your actions? What were others' feelings and why did they feel that way? How do you feel about this experience now?

✓ How does this situation connect with other experiences?

• How might the context of the interaction have constrained or enabled your actions and the actions of others?

• What was your role in shaping the dynamics of the interaction? In what ways have you influenced the behavior of others? How did you change the nature of the interaction?

Prepare for the Future and Apply Learning

✓ What insights have you gained from this experience, and what are their implications for the future?

✓ Does this situation require further action? Of what kind? Are there things you need to say or do? Are there knowledge gaps you need to cover? How can you validate your conclusions?

✓ Based on what you have learned, how are you approaching new situations?

• In preparing for future intercultural interactions, consider focusing on understanding situational factors as opposed to preparing scripts.

• During future intercultural interactions, consider asking yourself, "How am I contributing to the outcomes I am experiencing?"

Key Points

• Intercultural interactions do not happen in a vacuum. They happen within a cultural, organizational, and situational context.

• Intercultural interactions are influenced by three major components: individual differences in preferences, values, beliefs and skills; contextual demands and constraints; and intentional behavior, or the choices we make regarding how to deal with our intercultural situations.

- *Intercultural sensemaking* is the process by which individuals interacting within a social and physical context arrive at an understanding of what is going on, act based on this understanding, and in doing so further enact, or create, their situations.
- *Situational awareness* is the ability to consider the dynamically evolving context of an interaction while we are immersed in it.
- Context influences thinking and action in three ways: 1) it directs individuals' attention toward certain things and away from others; 2) it provides a system of meaning to interpret what is going on; 3) it limits the availability of behavioral options, thus influencing action.
- The context of an interaction is layered and includes the macro historical-political context, the cultural and institutional environment, the organizational context, and the situational context.

CHAPTER 4

Understanding Culture

Every story is informed by a worldview.

Brian Godawa, screenwriter

Intercultural interactions come in many forms and may result from the physical movement of people across cultural boundaries to live, study, work, or visit or from the increasing need to collaborate with others via computer-mediated communication. Cultural forces influence our work performance because we must confront different habits and work styles while we are abroad, deal with different perspectives and worldviews from our co-located and distributed team members, and make sense of news and commentary about people from other cultures we may not understand. As this chapter outlines, culture provides groups of people with the context in which interactions and behavior make sense and provides individuals with resources, skills, and preferred behaviors to deal with problems. In intercultural interactions, conflicts about values, norms, or interpretations may emerge. Identifying the best course of action is easier when we are aware of how culture influences *our own* behavior and understand the ways in which our worldviews are formed and how they influence what we do.

Before reading further, stop for a moment. Think about the culture or cultures you usually think of as yours. Make a quick list of assumptions, values, beliefs, or patterns of behavior you associate with your own culture.

How hard was it for you to describe your own culture? For many of us this exercise is very difficult. If you were not able to come up with any assumption or belief right away, you are not alone. Most of us are so strongly immersed in our own culture that we often fail to see how it affects our patterns of thinking and our behavior. The ancient Chinese Taoist philosopher Lao Tzu once observed that "water is the last thing a fish notices." Often, it is when we get out of our own culture that we become aware of our own cultural biases and assumptions, perspectives, obsessions, and patterns of action. Many of us take our own cultural upbringing for granted and assume that our thinking and behavior are just "common sense" and are widely shared or understood. I often start classes on cross-cultural or intercultural issues by asking a volunteer to explain his or her culture to an outsider. The most common answer I get is that the country in question (regardless if I am in Denmark, Belgium, Brazil, Canada, China, Colombia, or the United States) does not have a culture. Culture is usually something we attribute to other people, not to ourselves. While the term "culture" is highly visible in our popular discourse, it is often used loosely to explain social behaviors we don't understand. In this chapter, we focus on understanding culture and how it influences behavior within and across cultures.

Culture and Behavior

A search for the word "culture" on Google results in more than one billion hits referring to a wide variety of topics.[1] Academically, the concept has been approached in many different ways by many disciplines, and well over one hundred definitions can be found.[2] While culture scholars from all disciplines agree that culture is an important element influencing people's behavior, scholars have focused

Figure 4.1 Intercultural interactions

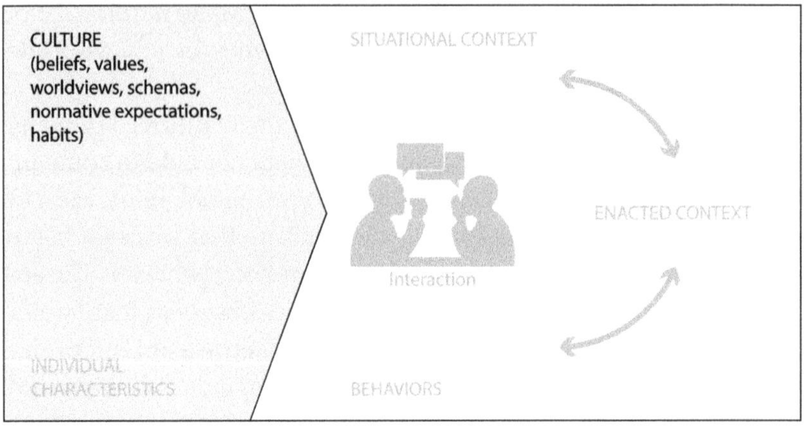

on different aspects of culture. For instance, scholars interested in comparing cultural groups tend to emphasize stable cultural dimensions that explain major differences in behavior *across* cultures (i.e., explaining why the Japanese in Japan behave differently from the French in France). Scholars focusing on explaining how individuals behave *within* a cultural context focus on how people use different cultural elements to assemble behaviors that are acceptable yet varied (how Japanese individuals behave differently yet consistently with Japanese culture). Depending on our needs, some of these aspects will be useful and meaningful. Both approaches are discussed below, with an emphasis on the role of culture in intercultural interactions as depicted in figure 4.1, a simplified version of the model presented in the previous chapter.

Culture and Collectives

Several scholars have approached the study of culture in order to understand how and why cultural groups differ from one another.

Three aspects of this approach to culture are particularly salient for the discussion here:

- *Culture is shared by members of a group* and often defines the membership of the group itself. Culture is what lies in between what is universally shared among people and what is idiosyncratic to individuals. Cultural beliefs, values, customs, habits, and preferences are shared by a group of people, even if not by all members of the group. The fact that spicy food is common in Korean and Mexican cuisine suggests that many individuals in these cultures are habituated to and/or like spicy food, but it does not imply that all of them prefer such cuisine, nor does it imply that all Dutch or Canadians dislike it.
- *Culture is learned through membership in a group or community.* The norms of behavior, values, assumptions, and habits of a culture are learned through immersion in that culture and observation of other acculturated members. We acquire values, assumptions, and behaviors by seeing how others behave, growing up in a community, going to school, and observing our family. Think about the acculturation process that happens when we join a new organization, as in going to university or starting a new job. To become one of "them," we receive training, observe others who have been members of that group for a longer time, and sometimes respond to explicit and implicit incentives to emulate them.
- *Culture influences the attitudes and behaviors of group members.* Culture tells us what behavior is acceptable and/or attractive and what behavior is unacceptable and/or unattractive. Culture defines the norms of behavior and puts pressure on members to accept and follow these norms. As a result, culture heavily influences how we see ourselves and what we believe and value. This, in turn, influences how we think those around us expect us to behave. This cycle further strengthens the role of culture in shaping behavior within a cultural community. As will be discussed later, when we are outside our cultural community, we may retain some components of our original culture but abandon others.

Understanding collective patterns of behavior within a cultural community and becoming aware of shared norms and values are very helpful when we join a new cultural community, as doing so provides us with a context to understand others and with ideas about how to fit in. At a collective level, cultural assumptions, values, beliefs, and behavioral norms are connected. That is, when we observe a behavioral pattern in a culture, we can typically find values, norms, and beliefs in support of that behavior. However, that is not necessarily true at the individual level, as individuals may subscribe to and incorporate the values and norms of their culture to different degrees.

Culture and Individuals

How much of our culture do we take with us when we move across cultures? When interacting with people from a different culture, do we behave the same way we do with people from our own culture? Existing research suggests that we behave differently in monocultural versus intercultural situations[3] and that most of us naturally and unconsciously adapt our behavior to adjust to new cultural environments, even though this adaptation may not necessarily make our behavior "better" or more suitable to the foreign culture.[4] Even though our cultural background may influence our interpretation of situations and our behavior, the context in which we are located plays an equally important role in shaping our behavior.[5] In other words, our culture influences our behavior when we are in an intercultural situation but not necessarily in the same way it does when we are within our cultural community.

Sociologist Ann Swidler's definition of culture is particularly helpful for understanding how culture influences the behavior of individuals in intercultural situations. She defines culture as a *toolkit* of symbols, stories, rituals, and worldviews that help the people of a culture to survive and succeed.[6] She argues that our behavior is *constrained* by our cultural resources, or the tools we can use, but *not determined* by them. If we think of culture as a toolkit, there is room for growth, for acquiring new tools, and for changing our behavior.

Let's take a closer look at the toolkit metaphor: contextual cues, such as a nail sticking up in a fence, interact with our mental models as we define what the problem is and select a tool (or solution) to deal with it. Our toolkit contains many different tools that might work, such as a hammer, pliers, or a hacksaw, but, over time, we develop a preference for – and become more proficient at – using one tool over others. This tendency is recognized in the adage "If you have a hammer, everything looks like a nail." Cultural tools are similar to a favorite hammer. Like the hammer in the adage, our favorite tools influence both how we define problems – the need to pound down the nail – and how we select solutions – the hammer.

Our tools are *logics of action*, or preferred ways of doing things. Our logics of action are mental models or ways of thinking that we can use in varying configurations to solve problems and get things done.[7] For example, if you were raised in a culture that sees direct communication positively, you are likely to be relatively skilled at direct communication, at saying what you think and "speaking up." You may use this skill or logic of action to deal with many different issues, such as disagreeing with your boss, negotiating with a spouse, or communicating with your child's schoolteacher.

Each one of us belongs to multiple cultural groups simultaneously, including our community, our profession, and perhaps multiple hobby or special-interest groups. We are multifaceted individuals and may be at the same time dentists, divers, and devout Buddhists. Each of these groups has its own culture with its own sets of values, beliefs, and norms of behavior. Our cultural makeup is thus layered and influenced by varied group memberships. The cultural layer that is salient can vary over time.[8] That is, while you are at the office your professional culture may be dominant, and when you are among your friends from church, the religious culture may be the most important. The notion that we belong to multiple cultures suggests that intercultural conflicts are not limited to the realm of societal culture but may happen within the same society across different cultural groups. Similarly, we may not experience cultural differences or intercultural conflict when interacting within a shared cultural group such as a professional organization. The culture that is salient to a group is the one that provides us with the context that helps us to know how to behave and what to expect of others.

Each one of us espouses cultural norms, values, and assumptions in different ways. Some of us subscribe more strongly to cultural traditions than others, and within a cultural community a range of behaviors are accepted and considered "normal." As a result, the same cultural behavior – such as celebrating Christmas – may be closely connected to values and beliefs for some individuals but be just a habit or even an obligation for others.[9] The notion that the influence of culture on behavior is not uniform and varies across individuals and situations suggests that it is not enough only to understand the cultures involved; it is also important to understand the aspects of culture that are called for in particular situations.

Culture and Situations

Culture influences our behavior differently across situations. Management scholars Kwok Leung and Michael Morris argue that cultural influences on behavior vary across situations depending on the degree to which *values, norms,* or *schemas* are most relevant to the task at hand.[10]

Cultural values are culturally influenced principles and judgments about right and wrong, and about what is desirable and undesirable. Values drive thoughts and behaviors in situations that call for ethical or moral judgments, such as a decision regarding whom to lay off or promote. Values are also prominent in situations where we do not feel pressure to adapt to others. For instance, in private and anonymous situations we may be inclined to follow our personal preferences and do not feel the need to comply with others' expectations. That is also true when the expectations of future interactions are low, such as an interaction with a one-off customer. We may also resort to our personal values in situations when we are clueless about how to behave. For instance, when abroad in situations where we do not know how to behave and norms are not clear in the environment, we may resort to behaving the way we think is right.

Cultural norms are behaviors that are typical and socially approved within a group. We learn cultural norms by observing how others behave and how others react to our behaviors. Cultural norms are particularly influential in situations in which others' evaluation of our behavior is important (e.g., a presentation to a customer or a job interview) or where deviating from norms may be sanctioned (e.g., may result in our losing a job or missing out on a promotion). Norms can be widespread within a society (e.g., shaking hands) or specific to a situation (e.g., a dress code). In ambiguous situations in which we do not have a preference or knowledge about how to behave, we are more likely to follow the norms we can observe in the environment.

Cultural schemas are knowledge structures storing information that guides interpretations, expectations, and responses. We filter the world through our schemas, which may be laden with cultural biases. Cultural schemas will have a greater influence on behavior when they are made accessible through environmental cues (e.g., cultural artifacts) or recent use. We rely on our cultural schemas when we are operating on automatic pilot and not considering other possible interpretations. For example, if I ask you now to imagine a "teacup," you may call to mind an image of teacup that is most familiar to you. However, when we deliberately think about situations we can recognize the limitations of our cultural schemas and call to mind alternative interpretations (you may recall different types and shapes of teacups you have seen from other cultures). Cultural schemas are more likely to be used when they fit the problem at hand, as novel problems are likely to force us into a sense-making process, as discussed in chapter 3.

Separating the different aspects of culture in influencing behavior helps us understand why in some cases migrants and expatriates are able to adapt to the *norms* of the host country without incorporating local *values*. It also helps us understand the ability of individuals exposed to more than one culture to switch frames of reference and behave differently in different cultural situations. These individuals

have multiple cultural schemas and can switch between them depending on the context in which they find themselves, such as following Indian norms of behavior in family situations but British norms in
work situations.

What this means for intercultural situations is that it is important
to consider which aspect of culture is salient in a situation. If the
situation at hand involves moral judgment – for example, a decision
regarding promotion – it is likely that cultural values will be most
important and play a role in how the interaction evolves. However,
if the intercultural situation is about normative behavior – such as
how to communicate in a meeting – we may be able to make situational norms clear and decrease ambiguity regarding how to behave. Furthermore, if the intercultural situation relies on people's
knowledge and interpretations – such as evaluating a behavior or
an artifact – cultural schemas may be called into action. These influences also depend on individual characteristics, as for some individuals the issue may be about values but for others it may be just
about schemas. Cultural self-awareness will help you know what
the issues are about for you.

Cultural Self-awareness

Cultural self-awareness is critical for developing intercultural competence, for two reasons. First, it allows us to compensate for lack of
cultural knowledge when trying to understand others. Second, it
helps us identify our boundaries and provides us with guidelines
for how to behave. I start by discussing the challenges associated
with learning about other cultures.

Learning about Other Cultures

The study of cultures is fascinating. It is amusing to learn about different, sometimes odd, habits and behaviors of people far away and
to have insight into the intricacies that help explain why a society

functions the way it does. It can also be disheartening when we realize how daunting the task of understanding other cultures can be. I am often asked, "How can I possibly understand all these other cultures?" The answer is very simple: You can't. For starters, we do not even know exactly how many cultures there are to be understood. If we start by looking at the number of countries, a very poor proxy for culture, we get to almost 200 countries in the world today.[11] This of course does not account for the significant cultural variations within regions and ignores cultural similarities beyond country borders. One alternative is to look at the number of languages spoken worldwide, as groups that maintain linguistic differences are also likely to maintain cultural differences. Linguists estimate that there are about 7,000 languages spoken in the world.[12] However, this approach still fails to recognize cultural variations within language groups, which can be quite significant (it would be inaccurate to equate Spaniards with Peruvians, French with Gabonese). Regardless of how we count cultures, it is clear that it is not possible for one individual to learn enough about all of them. So, what do we do?

A reasonable alternative is to focus on learning about a few dominant cultures that are relevant to you. That is, if you often work with Iranians, you learn about Iranian culture. This strategy has many benefits when it is possible to clearly identify the culture or cultures that are likely to have an influence in your life. For example, if you are going to Thailand to work for a Thai company with Thai colleagues, you can expect that the Thai culture will influence your work performance and quality of life. In that case, it will undoubtedly be helpful to acquire some understanding of the local language and culture. However, as was discussed in chapter 1, there are many situations in which cultural issues may not be so predictable and clear-cut, such as when we are working in a highly multicultural environment where it is not clear which cultures we need to know and in what context we will experience them.

A popular alternative to cross-cultural training used when it is not clear which cultures people need to know – such as in a university classroom or generic training programs – is to rely on generic

Table 4.1 Cultural themes[13]

Cultural Themes	Focus of Dimensions
Power distribution	Power distribution in organizations and society: The extent to which power and authority in a society are distributed hierarchically or in a more egalitarian and participative fashion.
Time	Organization and utilization of time: The extent to which people organize their time based on sequential attention to single tasks or simultaneous attention to multiple tasks; time as fixed versus time as flexible.
Social relationships	Role of individuals and groups in social relationships: The extent to which social relationships emphasize individual rights and responsibilities or group goals and collective action; the centrality of individuals or groups in society.
Social control	Relative importance of rules versus relationships in behavioral control: The extent to which rules, laws, and formal procedures are uniformly applied across societal members or are tempered by personal relationships, in-group values, or unique circumstances.
People and the environment	Relationship with the natural and social environment: Beliefs concerning how the world works; the extent to which people seek to change and control or live in harmony with their natural and social surroundings.

cultural dimensions as an entry point into culture. These generic cultural dimensions aim to provide universal themes with which to compare cultural groups, providing a framework for understanding major cultural variations. These cultural dimensions provide a shortcut to gaining a general insight into why some people think and act differently from others. These dimensions are a result of descriptions of cultures provided by an external observer seeking to find themes that apply across all cultures. The aim of this process is to identify cultural dimensions that are universally relevant and can be used across all cultures to describe and compare cultural groups. Several cross-cultural frameworks are available and have been widely used in research and teaching related to cross-cultural differences. A brief explanation of these themes as well as a brief review of some key cross-cultural studies is provided in appendix A. A summary of key cultural themes that have emerged across different studies is presented in table 4.1.

Cultural frameworks provide a useful overview of cultural trends across nations to help us make sense of our own and others' behavior. Seeing culture is difficult, and without some guidance concerning which values, assumptions, or behaviors are cultural, it may be difficult to notice the cultural differences that matter.

Cultural Reference Points

Consider the following: is a six-foot (183 cm) American man tall? Yes, if we compare him to average Americans, whose average height is about five foot nine (175 cm). However, if this man is also a professional basketball player, he would be considered to be short, as the average height in the National Basketball Association is six foot seven (201 cm).[14] What this example suggests is that descriptions and qualifications are only useful when put into context. From an objective point of view, we can say that someone is six feet tall (183 cm), but that gives us very little insight about whether this individual is tall or short unless we have a reference group in mind for comparison. It is the same with cultural descriptions. Descriptions and assessments of cultures are always made from a point of view, or in relation to another culture, just like our description of how tall someone is. When someone says that New Zealanders are friendly, Americans are ambitious, and Italians are passionate, that information comes with an embedded perspective or comparison group in mind – often the describer's, sometimes validated by a ranking provided by a cross-national study of culture. However, if we are not aware of the perspective used to provide the descriptions, they will not be very helpful.

As religion scholar James P. Carse has said, "To be prepared against surprise is to be trained. To be prepared for surprise is to be educated."[15] This notion is very relevant here because we can train people *against* surprise by helping them prepare for what they will experience in Nigeria or Vietnam. However, those of us who are constantly facing ambiguous intercultural situations need to be ready to be surprised. A good way to prepare *for* surprise is to understand our own culture and become fully aware of our implicit reference points (if you are five feet tall and come from a community where most people are about five feet tall, people who are five foot three may seem tall to you but short to others). Knowing our own culture is more than being competent in using the tacit cultural knowledge that helps us navigate everyday situations with ease, produce the right words at the right time, and get things done; being culturally self-aware means knowing our own values, beliefs, styles, and patterns of behavior and being able to *explain* them to others or recognize when they are not having the desired effect.

Let me share a personal example with you. As a Brazilian, I tend to enjoy animated, fast-moving conversations and am accustomed to the idea that five people may speak simultaneously and people will simply speak when they have something to say. In Brazilian culture, a good conversation has no pauses, only interruptions. I see interruptions as a sign of engagement and interest, thus am tempted to jump in and start talking anytime someone says something interesting. I now know that the meaning of interruption varies by culture and that some people may find interruptions extremely rude. Having this self-awareness, I am more careful when interacting with someone I do not know well. Depending on the situation, I will explain my interruption habit, try to suppress it, and/or try to remedy the damage after I have inadvertently interrupted someone inappropriately. I also search for ways to allow others to interject by pausing or asking questions if I notice I have been talking by myself for a while. When I meet someone new, I have no idea where they stand on the interruption-is-good / interruption-is-rude spectrum, but I know where *I* stand. Thus, I am prepared to observe, ask, and tell others about it. I can bring the subject to the table, and it no longer is a hidden source of misunderstanding. Can you think of a behavior you often engage in that has cultural roots?

Self-awareness allows for the consideration of the cultural basis of our own thinking and behavior and thus opens the door to new courses of action. When we know our culturally imposed limitations (e.g., belief that meetings should start promptly), we are better able to look for information to help us deal with situations as they arise. Learning about how our own culture has influenced our thinking and behavior also helps us to look at situations more neutrally. When we recognize that our ways of thinking are a product of our culture just as other people's ways of thinking are a product of their culture, it becomes easier to look at conflict neutrally and not expect that everyone will agree with our notions of what should be a universally applied best way of doing things. While learning enough about other cultures may be daunting, knowing about oneself is considerably easier and accounts for at least half of the problems in intercultural interactions.

Finding Our Boundaries

Self-awareness also helps us decide where our boundaries lie and how much we are willing and able to adapt to other cultures and situations. Intercultural interactions are fraught with differing views about what is good and bad, desirable and undesirable, appropriate or inappropriate. We are often put in a position where we need to decide whether we are willing and able to accommodate the needs and preferences of people from other cultures. You may have to decide if you are willing to take a job at an organization that has a highly hierarchical culture despite your more egalitarian preferences, or if you are willing to work with a colleague who is always late despite your preference for promptness, and so on.

As was noted earlier, behaviors and values are closely connected at the collective level but not necessarily at the individual level. Some of your preferences may reflect strongly held values while others may be based on habit or an expectation of what is common practice. You may be happy to deal with your tardy colleague but can't stand your centralizing boss, or vice-versa. As you identify cultural preferences, consider whether they are values, expectations that this is "the way things are," or simply things you never thought of before.

Also consider how the skills, habits, and perspectives you acquired through your cultural upbringing may be a resource to you. Through exposure to a culture, we acquire skills and perspectives that can both empower and constrain us. On the one hand, some of our perspectives may be difficult to let go of, making it difficult to adapt to a new cultural environment. For example, we may feel very strongly about performance-based promotions and find it difficult to adjust to a seniority-based culture. On the other hand, our cultural skills and perspectives may provide us with resources that are unique to us and instrumental in helping us succeed in our social and professional lives. For example, I find that having grown up in Brazil has equipped me with the ability to improvise and be flexible, which has served me well in many situations.

Towards Cultural Self-awareness

The exploration of our own culture takes time and effort. Culture is everywhere, influencing everything we do, think, or feel. Yet, it is easily taken for granted. Culture is embedded in the symbols surrounding us, our everyday rituals, the stories we tell, and the things we say, yet its prevalence often makes it difficult for us to see it. As discussed in chapter 2, reflection is a helpful tool for increasing self-awareness and helping us understand ourselves better. The practice of reflection allows us to notice patterns in our thinking and behavior and highlights themes we need to explore and issues we need to work on. As you do these reflection exercises, take the time to observe and examine your experiences and consider the symbolism, narratives, and rituals that are so much part of your everyday life that they may easily go unnoticed. Take the time to observe your culture and notice how it is influencing your thinking and behavior.

A useful way to explore our own culture is to take steps toward experiencing other cultures. Taking steps to stretch our cultural boundaries and experience new cultures helps us understand ourselves better. Consider the following reflection of a British woman living in Canada: "I'm not someone who swears a lot. Not in public, anyway. But what I've come to realize over the last week or so is that I probably have been swearing (to other people's ears) without even knowing it." She has realized that there are different expectations around swearing in Canada and Britain and noticed that her behavior was not having the desired effect.

When traveling is not possible, taking small steps toward exposing ourselves to experiences that are foreign to us but close to home, such as exploring activities with different ethnic or religious groups, can help us get out of our comfort zone and confront our taken-for-granted habits and expectations. Reading about our own culture is also a good way to gain insight into our values and beliefs. By reading about what others have to say about your culture you will notice two things: First, that cultural descriptions are often superficial. You will notice that they do not describe the whole picture, a great insight to apply when reading about other cultures. Second, information about your own culture provides a basis for thinking about whether these cultural characteristics resonate with you and in which situations. In other words, reading about your own culture provides good food for thought.

The Road Ahead

Culture has a pervasive effect on our thinking and behavior, often shaping our expectations, beliefs, values, habits, worldviews, and even skills. However, cultural influences on behavior vary across situations, and individuals subscribe to their own culture to different degrees. As a result, the influence of culture is unique to each intercultural interaction. Thus, we need to shift our attention to individual and situational factors that influence intercultural interactions and to behaviors that facilitate the creation of intercultural understanding. The next chapter discusses the role of individual differences in shaping intercultural interactions.

Reflective Exercise

This exercise asks you to reflect on your culture and how it influences your behavior across situations. You may choose to reflect upon a situation you encountered in a trip abroad, a work meeting, or any other situation in which you were faced with people from different cultures.

Tell Your Story

Write a detailed description of an intercultural situation. Draw on all your senses and make your description as rich and detailed as possible. What was the context of this situation? Who was there? What was influencing your behavior? What did you say or do? What did others say or do? How were you feeling?

Consider the cultures involved in this situation: Which national and organizational cultures were involved? How has culture played a role in this situation?

Revisit Your Story

Leave your story aside for at least one hour. Then, revisit your story by asking yourself the following questions:

- ✓ Are there facts, thoughts, or details not considered in your description that could change your interpretation of the story?
- ✓ What assumptions were guiding your actions? What knowledge might have influenced you?
- ✓ When interacting with others, what were you trying to achieve? Did you respond effectively? What were the consequences of your actions for others and yourself? What would be the consequences had you responded differently? What factors might prevent you from responding in new ways?

✓ How did you feel and why did you feel that way? How did your feelings influence your actions? What were others' feelings and why did they feel that way? How do you feel about this experience now?

✓ How does this situation connect with other experiences?

• What values or norms guided your behavior and your interpretation of the situation? Was your behavior normal for you? Was your behavior typical of others of your cultural background? Why or why not?

Prepare for the Future and Apply Learning

✓ What insights have you gained from this experience, and what are their implications for the future?

✓ Does this situation require further action? Of what kind? Are there things you need to say or do? Are there knowledge gaps you need to cover? How can you validate your conclusions?

✓ Based on what you have learned, how are you approaching new situations?

• In preparing for future intercultural interactions, consider if the issue is collective (e.g., developing a policy for operations in another country) or individual (e.g., discussing the policy with one individual).

• In preparing for future intercultural interactions, consider if the issue at hand is one of values, norms, or schemas.

• In preparing for future intercultural interactions, consider whether situational norms can be made clear.

• During intercultural interactions, consider whether there are other possible interpretations (different schemas).

Key Points

• At a collective level, culture explains why the behaviors of people are different across cultures. A community's culture is shared by its members; it is learned through membership and influences the attitudes and behaviors of group members. At the collective level, culture provides us with a context to make sense of behaviors.

- When interacting interculturally, individuals often adjust their behavior and may not behave in ways that are typical of their culture. At an individual level, culture works as a toolkit of resources that influences but does not determine behavior.
- Intercultural situations may be influenced by different aspects of culture. To understand the role of culture in an intercultural situation it is important to identify whether the problem is one of values, norms, or schemas. These influences may vary across individuals.
- Cultural self-awareness facilitates the development of intercultural competence by compensating for lack of knowledge regarding other cultures and helping us identify our boundaries.

CHAPTER 5

Understanding Individual Differences

Knowing others is intelligence; knowing yourself is true wisdom. Mastering others is strength; mastering yourself is true power.

Lao-Tzu, *Tao Te Ching*

People are different. What is acceptable to one person may not be to others, even within the same culture. Our personality, experience, and knowledge of other cultures, among other factors, influence the extent to which our behavior is typical of our culture as well as the extent to which we are flexible in accepting or tolerating behaviors that are not part of our culture. We do not need to go abroad to understand the importance of individual differences and appreciate the reality that understanding a culture in depth is never enough to predict others' behavior. Within our own culture, we are often puzzled by others' behavior and face disagreements, conflicts, and misunderstandings on a regular basis. When we add cultural differences to the mix, the challenges become harder to decipher because it is not always clear where culture ends and individual characteristics begin.

This chapter focuses on individual characteristics and intercultural interactions (see figure 5.1) for two reasons: first, so we can better understand how the cultural and situational forces discussed

Figure 5.1 Intercultural interactions

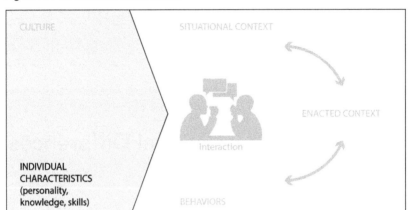

previously may play out differently depending on who is involved; and second, to increase our self-awareness and help us identify what we need to do to improve our intercultural competence.

Individual Characteristics and Intercultural Interactions

Psychologists have grappled for years with issues relating to the sources of individual characteristics and their implications for how individuals go about life and relate to other people. A discussion of the many ways in which individuals' unique characteristics may have an impact on their intercultural interactions is beyond the scope of this book. The purpose here is to highlight the fact that an intercultural interaction is as much *interpersonal* as it is *intercultural*. While there are many unique issues that arise because of cultural differences, there are others that are a product of individual characteristics and may or may not be associated with cultural differences. While some individuals can overcome cultural differences gracefully, others cannot. There are several factors that matter here: personality, knowledge and skills, sensitivity to context, and other traits that fa-cilitate intercultural interactions. These are discussed below.

Personality[1]

The *Big Five* framework of personality traits is often used for a brief depiction of someone's personality. Its five broad domains of per-sonality are as follows:

- *Conscientiousness*: The degree to which an individual is organized, careful, persevering, prudent, circumspect, and non-impulsive as opposed to disorganized, spontaneous, careless, prudent, and impulsive.
- *Agreeableness*: The degree to which an individual is pleasant, coop-erative, friendly, supportive, and empathetic as opposed to cyni-cal, confrontational, unfriendly, and mean-spirited.
- *Neuroticism*: The degree to which an individual is sensitive to neg-ative cues in the environment and prone to experience negative emotions such as anger, anxiety, and depression.
- *Openness to experience*: The degree to which an individual is open to new ideas, interactions, and environments.
- *Extraversion-Introversion*: The degree to which an individual seeks stimulation in the company of others and engages with the exter-nal world. Extraverts tend to be more talkative and enjoy social stimulation, while introverts tend to be more reserved and enjoy time alone.

Clearly, individual personalities influence how easy or hard it is for two individuals to get along. It is easier to deal with someone who scores high on agreeableness than with someone who is low on that dimension. Similarly, someone who scores high on openness to experience is more likely to be comfortable with different cultures, ideas, and ways of interaction.

Personality and culture have an interesting relationship. Personal-ity scholar Brian Little[2] suggests that individual personality comes from three main sources: our genetic disposition (*biogenic* sources), our cultural environment (*sociogenic* sources), and our individual plans, aspirations, and personal projects (*idiogenic* sources). This combination of genetic, cultural, and individual sources explains why we see variation in personality within cultures, while we see some patterns across cultures. For example, cultures may reward some personality traits more than others, such as extraversion in the United States[3] and introversion in Japan. As a result, individuals may become more skilled at activating cultural traits that are rewarded in their culture and become more proficient at them (sociogenic pressure). That is, we will observe more extraverted behavior among Americans than Japanese. However, our genetic disposition may predispose us to certain characteristics regardless of our culture (biogenic influence). Consequently, in a classroom environment it is often easier for Americans to speak up than it is for Japanese students. Still, there are always exceptions, as some American students will be introverted while some Japanese students will be extraverted.

In addition to genetics and culture, Little also added a third component of personality that is particularly relevant for intercultural interactions. He argues that people can activate personality characteristics in response to personal motivations. For example, a naturally disagreeable person may be motivated to please a potential client and "act out of character" by being highly agreeable during the interaction. Likewise, a natural introvert may be motivated to succeed in a project that requires extraversion. However, he points out that acting out of character may be exhausting, as it requires that we use additional resources to enact behaviors that are not "natural" to us. When required to act out of character, we may need to allow ourselves an opportunity to recover and recharge. For example, an introverted individual may need time alone after a day of active social interaction.

For our purposes, the important message of this line of research is that engaging in behaviors that are not part of our typical conduct is not only possible but may be essential during intercultural interactions. But it also points to the need for self-awareness and the recognition of our own needs in the long term. For example, those of us not naturally open to new experiences may need to make an extra effort to achieve the degrees of openness necessary to interact successfully with people from other cultures. At the same time, we should consider that to recharge and recover we may need to allow ourselves time to be immersed in highly familiar activities and situations. That may mean, for example, that after a day spent meeting clients in a foreign location we may need to retreat to our hotel room and watch familiar videos and eat some comfort food.

Intercultural Knowledge and Skills

The premise of this book is that we can, by acquiring knowledge and developing our skill in dealing with other cultures, influence and shape the process of an interaction in ways that facilitate understanding and collaboration. It follows logically from this premise that the knowledge and skills of the people interacting will influence to a great degree how interactions will unfold. For example, if you are interacting with a migrant from another culture who has been living and working in your own culture for several years, this individual may be very knowledgeable about your culture and able to interact in culturally appropriate ways, and you may not even notice any trace of cultural differences.

The length of time spent in a place is not, however, sufficient indication that people are acculturated in the specific domain we are dealing with. First, acculturation is seldom absolute. Even after many years, people may incorporate practices of the host culture and fit in perfectly in the work environment and public spheres but retain social values and assumptions from their own culture in more private realms. For example, it is not uncommon for perfectly acculturated professionals to choose to marry within their own culture and retain some aspects of their original culture at home. Second, individuals adjust to foreign environments in different ways.[4] At one extreme, some individuals choose to *separate*, trying to hold on to their home culture and refusing to adopt local practices and interact with the local culture, limiting their interaction with the host culture to the minimum necessary. These are expatriates who prefer to live in expatriate enclaves, do not learn the local language, and reconstruct a life that resembles the life they would have had in their home country. Individuals who adopt this strategy may have a difficult time building a rapport with the local community. For these individuals, interacting with locals will be an intercultural experience regardless of the amount of time they have lived in a place. However, depending on their job requirements they may very well be able to perform their duties satisfactorily. For example, an English teacher working for an American college abroad may be expected to keep her culture and behavior as part of her job.

At the other extreme, some individuals *assimilate* to the local environment and "go native." They let go of their original cultural habits and assumptions and incorporate the habits and assumptions of the new cultural milieu. Locals dealing with these individuals may find no cultural differences. In between assimilation and separation, some individuals employ an *integration* strategy and work toward retaining important aspects of their home culture while also building successful relationships in the new environment. While at first glance it may seem that integration is the best strategy and should be chosen by everyone, it is important to remember that host cultures vary in the degree to which integration is possible. Some environments, such as Canada, are open to multiculturalism and encourage integration, while in other environments the pressures to fit in are higher and people are forced either to assimilate or to separate. As you deal with migrants and expatriates in your own community, it is worth reflecting upon the pressures your culture places on them and the degree to which you expect them to assimilate, separate, or integrate.

When considering people's knowledge of other cultures, it is helpful to think about domains of cultural knowledge. As discussed in chapter 3, culture is acquired through experience in a community. We may be exposed to different cultures at different times in our lives. For example, through my experiences of growing up in Brazil, studying in the United States, and working in Brazil, the United

States, Belgium, and Canada, I have acquired cultural knowledge and skills based on my experiences in these countries. In some domains, such as how to interact with family members, my behavior is highly influenced by Brazilian culture. When dealing with academic matters, I am clearly North American. And while I have lived in Belgium for only two years, it was there that I had my only experience of being pregnant and a new mother. As a result, my cultural knowledge around pregnancy and birth is colored by Belgian cultural assumptions and practices.

In addition to our cultural knowledge, others' level of intercultural competence and ability to navigate intercultural situations will shape what we can do. If the other person is also engaged in shaping this interaction in productive ways, it will be a lot easier to find avenues for collaboration than if we must do all the work ourselves.

Sensitivity to Context

Chapter 3 discussed the importance of context in influencing people's behavior. However, individuals may be more or less sensitive to contextual cues. Some of us are chameleons; that is, we are highly aware of situational cues, and easily change our behavior to conform to the situations we are in, while others are less so and tend to behave more consistently across situations. In the psychology literature, this is referred to as *self-monitoring*.[5] High self-monitors are highly concerned with how others see them and attempt to comply with the norms and expectations of the situations in which they find themselves. Low self-monitors, on the other hand, are less concerned with others and tend to be guided more by their own values and beliefs than by the particular context they are in. I recently went to visit the Blue Mosque in Istanbul and decided to unscientifically explore this idea. The Blue Mosque attracts a large number of tourists from all over the world. On this particularly day, there were some Muslim tourists, many non-Muslim tourists, and some local Muslims saying their prayers. Observing the behavior of various tourists was very interesting. There was a large sign at the door of the mosque outlining the dress code: long pants for men, long skirts and hair coverings for women. Some tourists were dressed modestly, and some women respectfully put a scarf on their heads. Others were completely oblivious to the guidelines and, even when given a scarf, would not wear it.

My observations were unscientific, and I did not talk to visitors to try to understand why they did or did not wear a scarf. But I suspect there were two things going on. Some people did not *notice* they were expected to wear a scarf, despite all the signs suggesting they should. Some people are not good observers and may have taken for granted their own assumptions about what is appropriate attire. Others noticed the sign but *decided* not to comply with the request to wear a scarf based on their own values and principles: wearing a scarf went beyond their boundaries.

Some experts suggest that the ability to change behavior to fit new cultural situations is a critical component of intercultural competence.[6] But being a chameleon is not always the best answer. Sometimes, it helps to be able to modify our behavior to interact more effectively. At other times, it is best not to adjust to advance our goals. To behave effectively we need to know how much we can adjust to a new cultural context and identify where we will draw the line and stick to our principles. For example, two *non*-Muslim women may feel differently about wearing a scarf during a mosque visit on a sightseeing tour, when in a business meeting, or when visiting Muslim in-laws.

In intercultural situations, we need to be ready to make these types of decisions, and the lines are often murky and unclear. There is not one clear right or wrong answer to any of these questions, even if at times there may be wide agreement regarding a "better" answer or the most helpful behavior. Each one of us may come up with different answers and solutions at different points in time, based on our own values and beliefs and on the specific purpose and circumstances of a situation. The purpose of this book is not to tell you what to do in each intercultural situation you will face but rather to help you find your own answers. Consider: would you drink or not drink alcohol to comply with cultural norms abroad? In which situations? Would you change what you wear? In which circumstances? Would you eat or not eat certain foods?

These questions become relevant once you have noticed that you are in a situation that requires you to make the decision between adjusting or not adjusting. But how about those of us who have not even realized there was a decision to be made? The ability to notice that something is called for is clearly a prerequisite for good intercultural skills. Observation skills and sensitivity to context help us identify subtle cues in a new environment and give us a better understanding of our intercultural interactions. The development of these skills should not wait until we are facing a difficult intercultural situation in which multiple things are happening at the same time. Rather, it should be a well-polished skill by the time we need it. If you are not sure your observation skills are adequate, you may want to engage in some observation exercises, such as the following.

Observation Exercise

Stop for a moment and look around your environment, focusing your attention on as many details as possible. Now get out of this space, and write down as many details as you can remember. If you were reading in a very familiar space, such as your bedroom, try to remember non-obvious details such as what was on the bedside table, how much the curtains were open or closed, the position of the pillows on the bed, and so on. If you were in a public space, try to remember who was where and what they were doing (such as what the man in the green sweater was eating). Then go back to the space you have observed and check your notes. Were you right? Were your observations rich? Did you miss important details? If your list was short, try again after this second round of observation. Your list should get longer. You can do this exercise with anything that has lots of details, such as the picture on a book cover or the patterns on someone's clothes. The more you practice, the more details you will be able to capture.

Managing Identities

The context of a situation shapes not only the behaviors that are called for but *who we are* as well. Each one of us has many identities. We may identify as a man or woman or as a national of a particular country or a member of an ethnic, religious, or professional group. Those identities and memberships are fluid and become more or less salient depending on our social context. For example, our national or ethnic identity may become salient when it is unusual within a social context. This process of identification influences whom we see as similar to or different from us; whom we consider to be "us" and whom we consider to be "them." Thinking of ourselves as a member of a group or as an outsider is highly consequential because it influences how we think about others and how we act toward them. It also influences behavior because group memberships are associated with norms. As discussed in chapter 4, norms are standards for appropriate behavior. When an identity becomes salient, we are more likely to behave according to the norms of that social group.[7]

Our identity is the story we tell ourselves *about ourselves* as an answer to the question "Who am I?" Our identity is composed of attributes that we consider central and distinctive about ourselves. Our identity may include numerous attributes (I am smart, funny, kind, competitive, assertive, curious, and so on) that are constructed through social interactions in which we compare ourselves to others and define ourselves in relation to them. That is, we decide that we are kind, smart, athletic, or funny by comparing ourselves to other people. This self-categorization influences our behavior. For example, in a study of Filipino engineers in Canada, my colleagues and I found that some of our respondents would identify themselves as "engineers," others as "professionals," and others as "immigrants." These different categories influenced how they interpreted their skills, identified barriers to integration, and decided on professional and personal priorities. The categories also influenced their career decisions and their career outcomes. Individuals who thought of themselves as "professionals" or "engineers" were not willing to take menial jobs and were ready to move out of Canada if they did not find employment commensurate with their qualifications after some time. On the other hand, individuals who thought of themselves as "immigrants" were willing to take any job that would allow them to stay in Canada.[8]

This process of categorization influences not only how we position ourselves in relation to others but also how we act and how we feel about an interaction. For example, if you think of yourself as very articulate and communicative, you may feel much more frustrated and embarrassed when communicating in a language in which you do not have as much fluency as someone who does not think of herself as particularly articulate. Even though our identity is made up of multiple attributes, there are some identity components that are especially sensitive. Those refer to our need to feel competent, good, and worthy.[9]

Our own identity or self-image is closely linked to our interpretations of reality. In other words, we make sense of the world based on how we see ourselves. We tend to engage in activities that harmonize with our self-concept and associate with institutions that support our identities. When we are exposed to an idea or behavior that is at odds with what we believe, we may get defensive and think that other people's ideas or behaviors are nonsensical. One reason for this defensiveness is that our self-identities are threatened ("I am not this type of person"). For example, if you hold the belief that part of being a competent professional is to deliver your work on time, you may find it very difficult to deal with a multicultural team in which deadlines tend to slide. Accepting the sliding deadline contradicts your view of what is professional and makes you feel less competent. When we work with others from a different cultural background, our assumptions, values, and beliefs are often questioned, and consequently our perceptions about who we are – our competence, character, and self-worth – may be challenged as well.

For instance, in global business acquisitions, managers from an acquiring company are generally more powerful and have greater status than managers from the target company and may impose new rules and behavioral protocols on the acquisition. Individuals from a less expressive culture may be criticized for not smiling and engaging in small talk with customers and may feel their sense of competence threatened by new cultural rules. Having one's identity threatened can close off communication, impede learning, and eventually compromise the success of the relationship.

As part of developing intercultural competence, we need to develop *more complex identities* that can withstand the challenges imposed by intercultural interactions. Rather than looking at identity in terms of bipolar attributes ("I am competent/incompetent"), we need to develop a more multifaceted understanding of who we really are ("I can be perceived as competent in some circumstances but as incompetent in others"; "I can be compassionate and selfish, aggressive and accommodating"). We are all a mix of desirable and undesirable attributes, and we are not *always* performing at our best. In fact, we are not *always* anything. We can be very tolerant sometimes and at other times find ourselves not willing to accept certain views or behaviors. We may struggle to be as compassionate as we would like to be. And we may find that our sense of competence and security vanishes when we are facing a novel situation.[10] Self-awareness can help the process of constructing a more complex identity.

Self-awareness

Management writer Peter Drucker has advocated that success comes to those who know their strengths, values, and the ways in which they excel.[11] He argued that we can only produce results by focusing on our strengths and recommended that we seek answers to the following questions: What are my strengths? How do I work? What are my values? Where do I belong? What can I contribute? How do I work with people? When do I thrive? Drucker further argued that one of the secrets of effectiveness is to understand the people we work with so we can use their strengths. These questions are even more important in a culturally diverse environment because it is likely that we will see more variation in strengths, values, and work styles.

Self-awareness allows us to see ourselves in a more complex and comprehensive way and helps us understand the cultural and contextual components of our identity. Noticing and accepting our sensitivities – the issues that are important to us and define who we are – will help us identify when an *intercultural conflict is not about the other but about how we think of ourselves*. When our salient identity is threatened, we may revert to defense mode and consequently miss the opportunity to really understand the intercultural issues we are facing. Dealing with intercultural conflicts requires, first, dealing with oneself through reflexive dialogue. In other words, it requires addressing how the issue is reflected *inside our own mind* and how our sense of self is challenged or threatened by it. When we understand that our cultural background influences who we are, we are better equipped to separate our sense of worth from the situation.

The identity challenges posed by intercultural interactions are not necessarily a bad thing. In a positive sense, they open up possibilities and provide alternative ways of being of which we may not have been aware. On the other hand, the experience may be challenging, as questioning the things we know may lead to our feeling exposed and unsure. The belief that we know how things work – even if unwarranted – provides us with a foundation for action. When we realize our cultural limitations and learn about other perspectives, we widen our foundation of knowledge and repertoire of behaviors. However, at the same time we may have to reconstruct how we understand ourselves.

These changes may have a ripple effect. As we start questioning some taken-for-granted assumptions, we may face disruptions in our relationship with others from our own culture. As we start questioning our values and beliefs or when we hesitate to engage in behaviors that no longer fit our intercultural mindset (such as criticizing other cultural groups), we may face conflicts within our own culture. As we change ourselves, we influence others close to us. Our family and close friends may be faced with a new version of us that incorporates what we have learned from opening ourselves up to different cultures and ways of thinking. They may react to our behavior in different ways, may exert pressure for us to revert to our old selves – or they may change as well. As a result, this process of self-reevaluation and reconstruction may generate high levels of anxiety.[12]

Becoming Self-aware

There are several practical steps we can take to become more self-aware. As discussed in chapter 2, reflective journaling is one of them. A practice of regular writing and reflection helps us keep track of our thoughts, concerns, and experiences and, over time, can provide us with important insights into who we are. Formal assessments or tests may also be useful tools to help us learn more about our personality, cultural values, preferences, and so forth. Increased self-awareness may also be facilitated by talking to people close to us – people who understand us well and can provide us with feedback. Open and honest feedback from people we trust can help us notice and understand things about ourselves. I offer my students an exercise that is much appreciated.[13] I tell students to identify twenty people who know them well from a variety of different situations (e.g., family members, classmates, co-workers, friends). I then ask them to send a short e-mail to these people, inviting them to help with a personal developmental exercise by providing three stories of when the student was at his or her best. We ask for concrete examples so we can understand the situations and characteristics being described. The format of the examples should be something like this: "One of your greatest strengths is … For example, I think of the time that …" By requesting feedback from twenty people, the students often manage to get about ten responses back. Each respondent provides three examples, which gives thirty situations for students to analyze in order to better understand who they are. Perhaps you'd like to give it a try?

The Road Ahead

Intercultural interactions happen between individuals and are as much interpersonal as they are intercultural. Who we are and who we are dealing with matter as much as our cultural background, since we use our own knowledge, skills, and communication styles in intercultural interactions. Becoming aware of our own strengths, personality, and preferences is a critical step in developing intercultural competence. This chapter discussed the role of personality, intercultural knowledge, and sensitivity to context in shaping how individuals interact. However, who we are changes depending on the context, as some contexts create pressures to behave in certain ways and may override individual preferences. The next chapter discusses that in more detail.

Reflective Exercise

This exercise invites you to reflect upon your individual characteristics including your skills, personality, and culture. You have two options for this exercise. You can continue using the basic reflection guide or you can experiment with a variation that allows you to observe yourself from the outside.

Tell Your Story
Write a detailed description of an intercultural situation. Draw on all your senses and make your description as rich and detailed as possible. What was the context of this situation? Who was there? What was influencing your behavior? What did you say or do? What did others say or do? How were you feeling?

Consider: How have the individual characteristics of the people involved (especially your own characteristics) influenced this situation?

Variation: Fictional Story
Write your personal life story as if it were a story for a book, film, or play. You can choose to write about the past, telling the story of how you got to be where you are, or you can write about the future, imagining where you are going from here. Think about what type of story it would be: mystery, fantasy, romance, adventure, something else? Write the title of your story. Describe the main character (you)

in detail. What is the character passionate about? What are his or her talents? If you are writing a movie or play, identify an actor who would be appropriate to play you.

Choose a scene and write it in detail. How does the main character behave? What is he trying to accomplish? What is important to this character?

Have fun with this activity. Write as much as you like and set it aside.

Revisit Your Story

Leave your story aside for at least one hour. Then, revisit your story by asking yourself the following questions:

- ✓ Are there facts, thoughts, or details not considered in your description that could change your interpretation of the story?
- ✓ What assumptions were guiding your actions? What knowledge might have influenced you?
- ✓ When interacting with others, what were you trying to achieve? Did you respond effectively? What were the consequences of your actions for others and yourself? What would be the consequences had you responded differently? What factors might prevent you from responding in new ways?
- ✓ How did you feel and why did you feel that way? How did your feelings influence your actions? What were others' feelings and why did they feel that way? How do you feel about this experience now?
- ✓ How does this situation connect with other experiences?
- • What are your (or your character's) salient characteristics? Which of your strengths and weaknesses are visible in the story?
- • What guided your (or your character's) behavior? What was the role of culture, context, and individual characteristics?

Prepare for the Future and Apply Learning
- ✓ What insights have you gained from this experience, and what are their implications for the future?

✓ Does this situation require further action? Of what kind? Are there things you need to say or do? Are there knowledge gaps you need to cover? How can you validate your conclusions?

✓ Based on what you have learned, how are you approaching new situations?

• Consider situations and behaviors that are "not natural" to you (e.g., extraverted behavior) and consider how you can build recovery time into your activities (e.g., quiet time between meetings).

• Consider your intercultural knowledge and skills and their impact on your intercultural interactions. What do you need to learn to facilitate your interactions?

• Consider your sensitivity to context. How can you become more aware of your surroundings?

Key Points

• Intercultural interactions are also interpersonal interactions. Individual characteristics influence the degree to which individuals subscribe to their cultures and their ability to overcome cultural limitations.

• An individual's personality may facilitate or hinder intercultural interactions. Personality has three components: genetic makeup, cultural environment, and personal projects.

• Intercultural knowledge and skills influence the dynamic of an interaction by influencing what individuals can or cannot do.

• Individuals vary in how sensitive to context they are. Higher sensitivity to context facilitates intercultural interactions because individuals are able to notice subtle cues in the environment and act accordingly.

• Intercultural interactions may challenge our sense of self, especially our sense of competence, worth, and character. Developing intercultural competence requires the development of more complex identities.

- Self-awareness is critical in intercultural situations because our strengths, weaknesses, and work styles are varied and need to be negotiated. Dealing with intercultural situations often is about addressing how the issue is framed in our own minds.

CHAPTER 6

Understanding Situations

Look at situations from all angles, and you will become more open.

Dalai Lama[1]

Psychologists generally agree that human behavior results from a combination of individual characteristics and situations.[2] The physical and social setting of a meeting has the potential to affect our mood, cue in norms of behavior, and call attention to different problems and solutions. When we consider an intercultural interaction, the fundamental question that arises is the degree to which our surrounding circumstances impose demands and constraints that may be powerful enough to override personal and cultural preferences.

Imagine that you are organizing a meeting of several managers from different countries to discuss the future of your organization. Where should the meeting take place? Do you think it would be better to hold the meeting at headquarters, at a golf course in the countryside, or on the factory floor in the Chinese subsidiary? Who should be invited? How would you set up the meeting room?

Those decisions are important; they will define which norms, issues, and solutions become salient and, potentially, the social dynamics of the interaction. These decisions may exacerbate cultural

Figure 6.1 Intercultural interactions

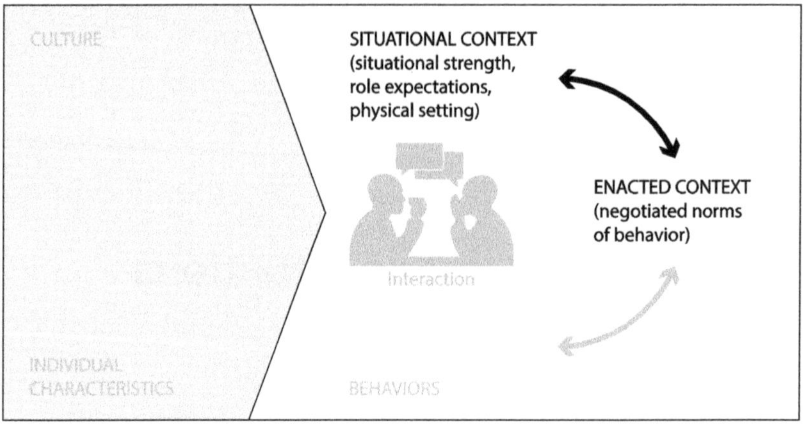

differences or make them unimportant. This chapter focuses on the circumstances surrounding an intercultural interaction and their influence on the intercultural experience (figure 6.1). It begins by considering the role of situational strength, or the power of situations to shape behavior.

Situational Strength[3]

Situational strength refers to the cues provided by the external environment regarding the desirability of potential behaviors. Strong situations put pressure on individuals to behave – or refrain from behaving – in certain ways. Because of this pressure, in strong situations there is less behavioral variability, and the influence of individual and cultural preferences or tendencies may be diminished. In many organizations, rules, procedures, and systems are designed to minimize the potential effect of individual shortcomings. These rules and procedures likely increase efficiency, as employees know exactly what to do. At the same time, these rules and procedures decrease the space for individual choice and may stifle creativity and initiative. On the other hand, in weak situations where the desirability of specific behaviors is not clearly established, individual and cultural differences are more likely to become salient.

The strength of situations is central to an understanding of intercultural interactions at work. First, some intercultural situations are *strong*, requiring specific cultural norms to be followed (such as when multinational organizations provide detailed guidelines for behavior). Second, situations may create an environment that facilitates or hinders understanding in ways that go beyond individuals' natural tendencies. The critical issue is to understand the ways in which a situation *may* override individual and cultural preferences and demand or cue in behaviors as well as allow certain characteristics to flourish and be expressed. For example, an individual may have high levels of cultural curiosity and would naturally seek to understand others and inquire about their culture – a behavior likely to facilitate understanding. However, the situational environment may suppress this behavior and make the expression of curiosity unsafe.

Psychology scholar Rustin Meyer[4] and colleagues suggest that the strength of a situation is the result of the *clarity* and *consistency* of behavioral expectations, the *constraints* imposed on behavior, and the *consequences* of behaving in ways that do not fit expectations. The impact of these dimensions on intercultural interactions is discussed below.

Clarity. In strong situations, behavioral expectations or requirements are available and easy to understand. For example, in an organization in which the dress code is clearly defined, communicated, and made visible, individuals are more likely to abide by the code despite their individual or cultural preferences. As individuals abide by a norm such as a dress code, the norm becomes even more salient and clear.

Consistency. "Consistency" refers to the compatibility of different requirements. In situations where various sources of information provide inconsistent guidelines (weak situations) people are more likely to rely on their own skills and preferences to decide how to behave. For example, if an organization has a written policy of equality in the workplace but some managers discriminate based on gender or ethnicity without consequences, individuals are receiving conflicting messages regarding the appropriateness of discriminatory behavior. In strong situations, various guidelines for behavior are consistent with each other.

Constraints. "Constraints" refers to the extent to which individuals' freedom to behave is limited by forces outside their control, such as limited discretion to deal with a problem. Constraints can be influenced by formal policies and procedures, behavioral monitoring systems, close supervision, and external regulations. In strong situations, there are limited choices of how to behave. For example, an organizational rule prohibiting the hiring of employees' family members coupled with a strong monitoring system may prevent this practice even when it is a local cultural norm.

Consequences. In strong situations, complying or not complying with behavioral expectations has important implications. For example, if employment depends on mastering the organization's host and local languages, employees are forced into bilingualism regardless of their individual preferences (or they will leave).

While situational characteristics create *demands* and *constraints* on our behavior, some people are more sensitive to contextual cues than others (see chapter 5), suggesting that the relationship between context and behavior is not the same for everyone. As we approach an interaction we need to consider culture, individual characteristics, and contextual factors *in combination* to identify the best course of action.

Like situations themselves (chapter 3), situational strength is a multilevel phenomenon influenced by societal, organizational, and situational factors. Societies vary in the degree to which non-compliance with rules and norms is tolerated as well as with regard to the consequences of non-compliance. Societies that rely on clear and rigid norms of behavior are typically referred to as *tight cultures*, while societies that tolerate a variety of different behaviors are referred to as *loose cultures*.[5] Situations encountered within tighter cultures may be stronger and provide individuals with fewer alternatives for action. For example, all women must wear a headscarf in public in Iran, regardless of individual and cultural preferences. If a meeting is taking place in Iran, the dress code for women needs to be followed regardless of the organizational culture and individual preferences.

Most organizational settings are somewhat strong because organizations, especially global organizations operating across several cultures, tend to have clear norms, rules, and procedures. However, even within organizations with strong cultures, behavioral expectations will vary across roles and physical settings. These are discussed below.

Role Expectations

We engage in multiple roles throughout our lives. On a given day we may enact the role of parent, child, friend, spouse, peer, customer, manager, teacher, community member, and so on. Depending on the roles we are enacting, we may think and behave differently. For instance, we will interact differently with our children than with our work colleagues. A police officer will interact with others differently in her role as a police officer than she does in her role as a member of the community.

Understanding the role that an individual is playing in an interaction is critical. Our location within the hierarchy and our assigned roles and responsibilities influence what is important to us, how we interpret facts and situations, and, as a result, how we behave. In fulfilling our roles, we become engaged in specific activities, procedures, and communications that determine which aspects of a situation become important to us. For example, a marketing manager may be most concerned with increasing the organization's visibility and reputation, while the finance manager may be most concerned with the cost of the initiative and the implications for the organization's bottom line.

Specific roles and positions in a social group also carry certain normative expectations.[6] These roles help shape people's interpretations of our approach to work and other people. For example, while we may expect to see the kitchen staff serving food or clearing tables in the company cafeteria, the same behavior by the CEO would likely catch our attention; it is "out of context." Normative expectations about roles may vary across cultures. For example, to what extent is it acceptable for a boss to go out drinking with the junior staff? Or to provide personal advice? Situational awareness implies not only an awareness of what my role is (e.g., a manager or teacher) but also an understanding of the *expectations* of others regarding what this role entails.

Because of these normative expectations, our role in an intercultural interaction guides what others expect from us and how they behave toward us. For instance, sometimes we go abroad with a specific purpose where our "foreignness" is our main asset, such as in situations where we are called in to train local personnel on a specific skill or process that is associated with our home culture. For example, consider Jack's situation.[7] Jack is an Anglo-American expatriate working for a U.S. company with South Korean business ties. Jack had a degree in East Asian studies, was fluent in Korean, and was passionate about Korean culture. When his employer needed an executive assistant to be located in Seoul to help manage the day-to-day administration of its joint venture and represent the American partner, he seemed like the perfect choice. He was easily able to mix with the local population and quickly embraced many of the characteristics of a typical Korean executive, including listening to subordinates' personal problems and keeping close ties with many of the men in the organization. However, his Anglo-American superior did not appreciate his adaptation to and assimilation into the local culture and soon started perceiving him as an adversary because he was not upholding the organization's culture and was becoming "one of the Koreans." The assignment was deemed a failure, and he was told to return to headquarters.

Jack's context was heavily influenced by the expectations of his managers in San Francisco. Jack was sent to Seoul as a representative of the American partner, and his adaptive behavior was not in line with the expectations associated with his role. Jack's situation also highlights the fact that sometimes people not participating directly in an interaction may have an important role in shaping our interactions.[8]

So, the questions in each situation become: *In this situation,* what is my role and how does my role shape the expectations around my behavior? The same questions apply to those with whom we are interacting. What is the role of my counterpart? Given his or her role, what are my expectations regarding how he or she will behave toward me? Are these roles clear or ambiguous? Are they fixed or dynamic? Are there conflicts regarding the roles we assign to each other or the expectations we have for those roles? As discussed in chapter 5, an intercultural interaction is influenced not only by the roles and positions of the players or participants but also by how they enact their roles and positions based on their skill sets, beliefs, values, and personal characteristics.

The expectations that others have of us are not only based on our job titles. As discussed in the last chapter, our identities are based on the social groups to which we belong. These identities are visible to others, so that we may be seen as "the woman," "the accountant," or "the immigrant" in the room. Characteristics such as gender, age, accent, ethnicity, clothing, or other physical characteristics may influence the way people are perceived and expected to behave and, consequently, the way they interact with others. These expectations may be positive or negative, helpful or unhelpful. Often they are based on stereotypes. Stereotypes are simplified mental representations we have of other groups of people. When discussing stereotyping in the context of intercultural interactions, we usually emphasize the need to see beyond stereotypes – which is clearly important. However, we also need to consider that sometimes *we* may be seen through stereotypes without realizing it. Just as it is important to control our urge to stereotype individuals based on various characteristics, it is important to be prepared to deal with the stereotypes people may have about us and proactively address any misrepresentations or incorrect assumptions.

Physical Setting

The physical setting in which an interaction takes place can have a profound impact on the nature of an interaction and its outcomes. The location of work, negotiations, or meetings often influences the social dynamics by affecting frames of reference, stress levels, and topics of conversation. Consider how different it is to work in a library as compared to a coffee shop or to have a meeting in a pub as compared to a formal boardroom. The physical setting, including its geographic locale and the characteristics of that locale, influences people's perceptions and provides cues as to what is important and what behaviors are expected. For example, a meeting at headquarters is more likely to focus attention on company needs and home country rules, while a meeting at a foreign subsidiary is more likely to focus attention on the local culture and needs. A plant location is more likely to make manufacturing issues salient, while an off-site meeting may invoke new ideas. This explains the popularity of organizational retreats, where employees are taken to an off-site location to discuss issues. An off-site meeting may call for more informal interactions and relax some behavioral expectations. It is also a reason why meals and coffee or tea breaks are such a major part of business and professional meetings, providing opportunities for participants to connect and interact with each other in more informal and personal ways.

As discussed in chapter 4, we belong to multiple cultures, and multiple cultures coexist within organizations and nations. The cultural layer that is salient varies over time in response to the situational context, which provides members with specific behavioral guidelines for each situation. For example, an individual may be Japanese, an accountant, a computer gamer, and a sailor. Each of these memberships is associated with a culture or subculture that guides the behavior of members. We have a repertoire of possible behaviors and, when interacting with one another, we rely on situational cues to determine the type of situation and which culture is dominant. Oftentimes the organizational culture is more important than the national culture when we are dealing with co-workers across the globe. In other words, we use our environment, such as the office or a sailing boat, as a clue to which cultural rules apply and to how we are supposed to behave.

The way furniture is arranged also helps us figure out what behaviors are expected. Studies on office design suggest that the physical setting of an office can improve collaboration and problem solving between groups, influence people's attachment to their workplace, and signal status and group membership. For example, the presence of a whiteboard facilitates brainstorming and collaboration, the way boundaries are placed between groups influences the amount and types of interactions between people, and the ability to personalize office space helps people establish their personal boundaries and affirm their individual and group identities.[9]

The ways in which we use our space and position ourselves in relation to others communicate to others how we feel. The study of how humans use space (called *proxemics*) is well developed, and a discussion of the subtle details of the use of space, body angling, and positioning is beyond the scope of this book. Generally speaking, the closer we are to each other, the more informal and friendly the relationship. However, what is considered a comfortable distance varies widely by culture. The distance that is considered intimate for a Finn may feel formal and cold to a Spaniard.[10]

Think about how where we sit provides clues about our interest and willingness to collaborate. In a library or canteen, you may sit diametrically opposite someone to signal you are not interested in getting involved in a conversation. At a square or rectangular table, sitting side-by-side with someone invites more collaboration than sitting opposite, as a desk in the middle acts as a shield or defensive mechanism. King Arthur's idea of using a round table was to give each of his knights an equal amount of power and status. At a round table, people can claim the same amount of space and see each other easily, an arrangement that may help promote discussion and collaboration. (King Arthur may not have allowed for the fact that his own position at the round table would influence the dynamics of the conversation, as people closer to him would be considered more important than those seated farther away.)

While the physical location and furniture arrangements matter, in some situations they are more important than in others. Some situations require that we monitor our behavior more closely,[11] suggesting that we are likely to be very sensitive to all physical cues around us. For example, if you are participating in a job interview or appearing in court, you are likely to be very attentive to your behavior and to all cues as to how you are supposed to behave. If you are in the company of intimate friends and family, however, you may act more naturally and be less constrained by your environment.

Managing Intercultural Situations

When we think about our context and situations, we often assume them to be objective, material, and independent of us. For example, when we are trying to understand another cultural group based on our observations, we may ignore the fact that our presence is an integral part of the context being observed and that the people in question are reacting to our presence. For example, when I am teaching in Shanghai or Bogota, I am influencing the behavior of Chinese and Colombian students. They are reacting to my presence and to their expectations about what a Brazilian professor teaching for a Canadian university expects, knows, and does. Also, let's not forget, they are required to speak English when I am around, which changes the dynamics of their interactions. In other words, *my* presence is an integral part of *their* context.

In addition, when attempting to understand the behavior of another group we are filtering from multiple stimuli in that environment, focusing on some aspects of it and ignoring others. As well, we are creating and acting on interpretations based on the things we selected for attention, and so are further shaping our experience. The bottom line is that while our context (where we are, what we are doing, who is there, and so on) is a very important influence on how our interactions evolve, we are an integral part of the context we are experiencing.

As tempting as it is to assume that the context around us is happening *to* us, and we are just witnesses to it, the reality is that even if we are just observing, we are having an impact on what other people do. *Our role, power, goals, and characteristics are an important contributor to the way the situation is evolving.* In some situations, our impact may be rather small. For example, when observing the behaviors of others in a public place we may go unnoticed. However, at other times our influence may alter the context significantly, such as when we are visiting an organization as a topic expert. Recognizing how our actions are shaping or can shape a situation by structuring the attention, interpretation, and behavioral patterns of others is critical to developing intercultural competence.

Structuring Attention

We experience life as a flow of ambiguous stimuli. To cope with this ambiguity, we break up our experience into small portions to which we attach categories. We may think of our day as made up of discrete events and situations (I went to work, I had a meeting, I had lunch, and so on) as opposed to a continuous flow of experience. This process of *bracketing*, or selecting parts of our experience for attention, gives shape to our experience and modifies our interpretations and interactions.

Stop for a moment and consider all the stimuli around you at this moment. You may be feeling the texture of the chair on your back and thighs. You may be hearing all sorts of background noise, feeling the room temperature and the contact of the book or digital device on your hands, smelling the aroma of coffee or the scent of flowers, and so on. However, you may ignore most of these stimuli and think of your present circumstance as "taking a work break," "waiting for my flight," "going home," or "doing my homework." To cope with the multitude of stimuli and facilitate sensemaking, we tend to simplify our experience into chunks.

Our intercultural interactions are just as ambiguous and dynamic. What becomes salient to you is *not necessarily* the most important part of an interaction from another person's perspective. The old adage of seeing the glass as half empty or half full is a good example of how different people will see different things when facing the same situation.

The first step toward creating better intercultural situations is to become aware of our own attention patterns. We need to consider whether there are other components in the interaction that, if taken into account, would help us understand the situation differently and enable us to behave more effectively. There are numerous things one could focus on during an intercultural interaction, and it would be impossible to list all of them. As an example of how what we focus on changes how we behave, let's consider the issue of focusing on the differences or similarities of people across cultures, as this is a topic of heated debate among world travelers and interculturalists.[12] Some people argue that there are some universal characteristics that are shared by all humans and that paying too much attention to cultural differences between people creates unnecessary boundaries and separations. This view suggests that if we can get past our cultural differences and draw on our common humanity, we will be fine. On the other hand, others argue that overlooking cultural differences brings important risks and unnecessary conflict. These people emphasize the fact that there is a fundamental difference between growing up in Tehran, Rio de Janeiro, Tokyo, or Vancouver, and to say that those differences have not impacted people's worldviews and behaviors is naive. Others still will argue that we need to focus on our differences as they provide opportunities for creativity and synergy.

All three views are correct. We are at the same time similar and different, and our differences and similarities are a source of both conflict and synergy. There are times when we need to focus on our differences so we can understand each other better and benefit from the variety of views and resources our different backgrounds bring to the table. However, at the same time, we need to keep sight of the similarities between people so we do not fall into the trap of creating an artificial "us" versus "them" dichotomy. At any point in time, however, our focus on differences or similarities will shape our interactions by drawing our attention to different aspects of our intercultural relationship.

When we consider the possibility that contexts are not fixed and uniformly perceived, we open the door to multiple perceptions of the same context. Each of us may notice and focus our attention on different aspects of a situation and, as a result, may interpret the situation differently. I once witnessed an interesting example of this phenomenon. When teaching negotiation techniques in Denmark, I assigned an American and an Austrian student a meeting room to work on a role-play exercise. The American entered the room and sat down in the first chair he came to. The Austrian student noticed that her counterpart sat in the higher chair in the room and interpreted this action as an attempt to assert power. She concluded that the American student was not being sufficiently collaborative and decided to play tough. The American, unaware of the difference in chair heights, noticed that his colleague was being difficult, maybe even unreasonable, and decided that she could not be trusted. They did not reach an agreement. When we discussed the outcome of their experience, the Austrian student kept referring to the height of the chairs, to the bewilderment of the American student, who had not noticed anything special about the chairs. The salience of the chair height to the Austrian student may have been a result of an *expectation* that the American student would be aggressive, which in turn made salient cues in support of her expectations. For the American, the chairs had no meaning and went unnoticed.

We have the *potential* to influence how others understand a situation by altering the objective context of an interaction (e.g., changing the height of our chair) or by influencing others' perceptions of the context (e.g., openly referring to the fact that we inadvertently chose the higher chair). Physical artifacts and symbolic behaviors are powerful tools for structuring attention. When we introduce or eliminate artifacts and symbols or modify the physical arrangements, we may influence what becomes salient and how others interact with us. For example, placing a bowl full of apples in a room with a table and chairs will have a different impact than placing pads of paper and pens. Similarly, by drawing attention to specific aspects of the overall experience, we can help transform what may be a complex and ambiguous field of activity into something discrete and imbued with meaning. For example, by calling attention to features of the context that we think are important, such as the multicultural nature of the team, we may deflect attention from any local cultural norms.

Understanding the role of attention in behavior helps us improve our intercultural interaction in two ways. First, by being mindful of what we are focusing our attention on and questioning whether we are ignoring important aspects of the situation, we may be able to identify better behavioral choices. Second, we can attempt to influence what others focus on by using verbal communication or symbols and artifacts to call attention to some characteristics of the situation they may have ignored.

Structuring Interpretations

Even when we notice the same things, we may interpret them differently. Labeling is a key process in interpretation. When we categorize and label an object or experience we call in a mental schema with information about that category or experience. Schemas are cognitive structures in which our knowledge is retained and organized.[13] Our schemas guide our process of "What is it?," "What does it mean?," and "How should I respond?" The labels we use are critical in determining our experience, as they activate a set of expectations, interpretations, and actions. Consider the following passage:

> The procedure is actually quite simple. First, you arrange things into different groups. Of course, one pile may be sufficient depending on how much there is to do ... It is important not to overdo things. That is, it is better to do too few things at once than too many. In the short run this may not seem important,

but complications can easily arise. A mistake can be expensive as well. At first the whole procedure will seem complicated. Soon, however, it will become just another facet of life.[14]

Can you comprehend the passage above? What if the title was "washing clothes"? When we have a context or a label, it is easier to make sense of information. Now, for contrast, reread the passage above considering the title "Organizing Receipts for Tax Purposes."[15] When we label an experience, we cue in a specific schema, which shapes our interpretation process. Research suggests that the way we label or categorize an object, person, or experience has an important role in shaping our expectations and judgments. Studies of mental product categories suggest that the way we categorize new ambiguous products will influence the expectations we have of this product. For example, when digital cameras were introduced, consumers who categorized them with film cameras had higher expectations regarding picture quality than those who categorized them with computer equipment.[16]

Through the same process, ambiguous situations take shape and form once we attach labels to them and, as a consequence, associate them with expectations, judgments, and meaning. The meaning of a behavior we experience will change if we change the labels we use. If we label an individual's behavior as "rude," we will treat the person differently than if we label the person's behavior as "different." As a consequence, the words we use to describe a person or experience are critical in influencing the dynamics of the evolving situation. In the process of an interaction, we need to be mindful about *our own categorization processes*. We may label and categorize our experience in multiple ways, and multiple meanings may be attached to the same experience. For example, you may think of your meeting as a way to interact with your colleagues, a necessary part of work, or a waste of your time. Depending on how you think about it, you will behave differently. Others, in turn, will react to your behavior in a process that resembles a self-fulfilling prophecy. If you think about an interaction as difficult, you may act in ways that make the interaction more difficult than it needs to be.

Understanding the role of labeling and categorizing in influencing how people interpret situations has important implications for understanding the way we interact with others. First, we need to be mindful of the way we are labeling and categorizing ourselves, others, and the behaviors and situations we face. What would change if we labeled it differently? Why did we choose this label? Is there a more encompassing and inclusive label? Second, we need to be mindful of the interpretation processes of others and choose our words carefully. We may focus on understanding how they are seeing the situation and look for ways to convey our own understanding. We may proactively frame our communication, providing people with labels and categories to emphasize a subset of aspects of a situation or issue.

While sometimes we may have a significant influence on how a situation is understood, we have to account for the fact that "power privileges some meanings over others."[17] In other words, when people are attempting to reach a shared understanding, some participants have more power than others in defining interpretations. Sometimes this power is based on their position in the hierarchy (the boss's interpretation is the one that prevails), but often we see that some people have more legitimacy, or *symbolic power*, and through this power are able to define a situation.[18] That is, people with symbolic power are able to generate interpretations that others embrace in ambiguous situations. We tend to attach more (or less) weight to the interpretations of people on the basis of their personal characteristics, connections, and status.

Following this principle, success in intercultural interactions depends not only on how adaptable we are but also on the *extent to which others embrace our definition of the situation*. In other words, success in intercultural interactions is dependent upon the degree of symbolic power, or the power to define the situation, that different people have. When we are aware of our symbolic power – or lack thereof – we may engage in purposeful activities to influence meaning creation or to attain symbolic power. In an intercultural situation, this may require explaining behaviors that usually do not require explanation and imbuing them with meaning. For example, a manager who tends to speak informally and disregard titles may explain that the behavior is meant to demonstrate that the value of an individual is based not on the person's position but on his or her contributions. By explaining her behavior, she assigns meaning and helps others make sense of potential discrepancies caused by her behavior.

Structuring Action

Recall that intercultural competence is the ability to influence or shape the process of intercultural interaction in a way that creates opportunities for cooperation. So far, we have discussed what goes on in our minds when we are faced with cultural discrepancies. At some point these interpretations will be reflected in our actions as we decide what to say, how to dress, whether to extend our hand for a handshake, or whether to ask or not ask a question. The questions to consider here are "What can I do?" and "How can I positively influence the behavior of others?"

The first issue to consider is the degree to which the situation we are facing is already "strong" and whether clear rules and guidelines regarding how to behave are present. When clear guidelines are in place, our options may be limited. However, many intercultural situations are "weak," with unclear or undefined rules, and we may be able to influence behavior positively through the articulation of rules. For example, if you expect people to take their shoes off when entering your home, you might make that norm explicit through signs ("no shoes please"), artifacts (shoes at the door), or clear instructions ("please take your shoes off").

Sometimes we can tell people what to do, or ask people what to do ("Should I take my shoes off?"), but at other times we need to *negotiate norms of behavior* through interaction. For example, to work with others, we need to agree about timelines and expectations of promptness. How late is too late? For instance, we may agree that in our specific context and considering the purposes of our interaction, fifteen minutes is not considered late, but that further delays should be avoided – or at least deserve an apology. Alternatively, we may agree on a clearer specification of time when making appointments: 8:00 a.m. Mexican time typically means that delays are accepted, while 8:00 a.m. British time typically means that punctuality is expected. These rules should cover the most important cultural obstacles to the success of the relationship, whether they are about time, the use of titles, or styles of communication.

Understanding the role of cognitive processes in influencing action is important for interacting effectively in intercultural situations. First, it highlights the importance of being mindful of our own behavior and its implications: Why am I doing what I am doing? Am I operating on autopilot and following my taken-for-granted assumptions about what is the right thing to do? Does my behavior require explanation? Is there a better way to achieve my goals in this interaction? Second, it helps us see how we may be able to influence other people's behavior by making behavioral expectations clear.

The Road Ahead

Intercultural interactions are influenced by cultural and individual differences in preferences, values, and beliefs; contextual characteristics and their consequent demands and constraints; and intentional behavior, or the choices we make regarding how to deal with intercultural situations. Situational awareness involves understanding these pressures and also connecting with the other person (or persons), sensing what others are experiencing, and appreciating the meaning they give to their experience. This requires understanding not only who they are, their roles, their goals in a specific situation, and the type of relationship we are able to develop, but also how *we* are shaping and influencing the situation in which we find ourselves. Our situations influence our behavior in varying degrees by establishing *demands* and *constraints*. However, within these limitations, we typically have *choices* about what to do and how to do it.[19] This is where our intercultural skills and communication abilities take center stage, as will be explored in the following chapters. The emotional side of intercultural interactions is discussed in the next chapter.

Reflective Exercise

This exercise invites you to become aware of the influence of situations on your behavior, increasing your situational awareness.

Tell Your Story
Write a detailed description of an intercultural situation. Draw on all your senses and make your description as rich and detailed as possible. What was the context of this situation? Who was there? What was influencing your behavior? What did you say or do? What did others say or do? How were you feeling?

Consider details of the physical and social setting surrounding the situation. What were the physical properties of the location? What types of furniture or artifacts were visible? What were their function and meaning in the environment? How did people interact with those elements? Who was present in this location, and what were their roles? Were there other people not present but influencing the interaction? Which factors were most significant in shaping your experience? Did you alter the context in any way? How?

Revisit Your Story
Leave your story aside for at least one hour. Then, revisit your story by asking yourself the following questions:

- ✓ Are there facts, thoughts, or details not considered in your description that could change your interpretation of the story?
- ✓ What assumptions were guiding your actions? What knowledge might have influenced you?
- ✓ When interacting with others, what were you trying to achieve? Did you respond effectively? What were the consequences of your actions for others and yourself? What would be the consequences had you responded

differently? What factors might prevent you from responding in new ways?

✓ How did you feel and why did you feel that way? How did your feelings influence your actions? What were others' feelings and why did they feel that way? How do you feel about this experience now?

✓ How does this situation connect with other experiences?

• In what ways did the context enable or hinder this interaction? Did you respond effectively, given the context?

• Could you have had a positive influence in this context? Did you? What could you have done to make other people's experience of this context better?

Prepare for the Future and Apply Learning

✓ What insights have you gained from this experience and what are their implications for the future?

✓ Does this situation require further action? Of what kind? Are there things you need to say or do? Are there knowledge gaps you need to cover? How can you validate your conclusions?

✓ Based on what you have learned, how are you approaching new situations?

• What are some ways in which you can facilitate understanding by calling the attention of others to different aspects of your relationship?

• What are some ways in which you can facilitate understanding by framing your communication and facilitating the development of a common understanding?

• What are some ways in which you can alter the characteristics of your environment to make behavioral expectations clear?

Key Points

• Behavior results from a combination of individual characteristics and situations. Thus, the characteristics of a situation are critical in defining how an intercultural interaction evolves.

• *Situational strength* refers to the cues provided by the external environment regarding the desirability of behaviors. Strong situations put pressure on individuals to behave in a certain way and may override individual preferences.

- The strength of situations is a result of the *clarity* and *consistency* of behavioral expectations, the *constraints* imposed on behavior, and the *consequences* of behaving in ways that do not fit expectations.
- *Role expectations* refer to expectations we have based on the roles individuals have in an interaction.
- The *physical setting* of an interaction provides cues regarding norms of behavior, salient issues, and the relationship between people.
- We are an integral part of our situations, and our behavior shapes the contexts in which we are immersed. We may influence situations by calling attention to some characteristics of a situation and away from others, by providing people with labels and categories that emphasize a subset of issues, and by making behavioral expectations clear.

CHAPTER 7

Managing Feelings

But feelings can't be ignored, no matter how unjust or ungrateful they seem.
Anne Frank, *The Diary of a Young Girl*

Intercultural situations have the potential to elicit strong feelings. On the positive side, we may feel interested in or fascinated by new ideas, inspired by new ways of living, and hopeful about the possibilities of the interaction. More negatively, we may feel vulnerable because we do not understand what is happening and we are not sure whom we can trust. We may feel wronged and start questioning our competence and worthiness. We may feel uncertain, vulnerable, and anxious, because we believe we are not in control of our situation, cannot understand what is happening, and cannot predict what other people will do. Positive feelings support our interactions, broaden our mind, and facilitate cooperation. However, negative feelings make it difficult to be open and receptive to new ideas and points of view.

As Ann, a Chinese graduate student, confided, "I always feel nervous when talking to North Americans because I don't know how I can get to know them personally without offending them by asking too many personal questions." The realities imposed by the new interactions (should not ask personal questions) and the expectations based on our own cultural background (I need to know them personally) create a sense of disequilibrium that can lead to feelings of anxiety, stress, and confusion. In the context of living abroad these feelings are normal manifestations of what is known as *culture shock*, a disequilibrium caused when an individual's internal capabilities are not aligned with the demands of a new cultural environment.[1] Similar feelings of confusion, otherness, and anxiety can be experienced at home when interacting with people who are different from us. Working in a diverse environment may generate a state of successive micro-cultural shocks that leave us feeling uncomfortable and may curtail our ability to interact positively.

The development of intercultural competence requires high levels of *emotional literacy*.[2] Emotional literacy involves emotional self-awareness, which is the ability to recognize feelings when they emerge; being able to separate feelings from actions; working with our feelings, including tolerating feelings of frustration and fostering positive feelings; and empathizing with others, reading their emotions, and responding appropriately. This chapter explores the feelings associated with intercultural interactions and the cultural roots of emotions. It then discusses avenues for working with our feelings in the course of an intercultural interaction.

Intercultural Interactions and Feelings

Intercultural interactions may elicit feelings of uncertainty, ambiguity, and anxiety. We are confronted with *uncertainty* when we are unable to predict or explain the behavior of others.[3] To be successful in an intercultural situation, we may need to behave differently from usual, but it may not be clear what that behavior is. For example, consider the uncertainties associated with joining a new community or starting a new job. The first time we engage with a new community, even within our own country, we may not know what to expect or how to behave. We experience *ambiguity* when we are unable to make sense of or interpret facts and situations. As we engage with individuals from another culture, we may be unable to interpret the meaning of their behaviors. For example, imagine that someone does not respond to your e-mails. Until you know more about this individual and her circumstances you may not know how to interpret this behavior: is it a technological problem? Is it that she does not want to communicate with you? Or is it that she just does not reply to messages promptly and you should telephone instead? We experience *anxiety* when we are uneasy or apprehensive about what will happen when we interact with people from other cultures.[4] The uncertainty associated with the inability to predict behavior and the ambiguity associated with the inability to interpret and respond to situations may result in heightened anxiety and frustration.

Managing the feelings that arise in intercultural situations is important for two reasons. First, because intercultural learning is an emotional process. The way we feel about a person, situation, or ourselves is critical in guiding what we can or cannot learn from it. Second, because our actions are influenced by the way we feel, our emotional state influences how we communicate, how we interpret the situations in front of us, and how we choose to behave. When we feel angry or frustrated with someone it is harder to engage in constructive behavior. The first step toward managing feelings is to become aware of them.

Emotional Self-awareness

A prerequisite for the development of intercultural competence is the ability to recognize, acknowledge, and process feelings.[5] However, being aware of our own feelings is harder than it might seem. Most of us are not aware of the complex and nuanced feelings we experience. We may recognize some dominant emotions ("I am angry"), while failing to notice many subtle, contradictory feelings (frustrated, betrayed, embarrassed, regretful, unworthy, abandoned) that may quickly be transformed into judgments (if he was competent he would show up on time), attributions (she is trying to hurt me), characterizations (he is inconsiderate), and conclusions (she needs to says what she means). Notice that those statements may seem to express *feelings*, but they do not indicate whether we feel angry, frustrated, or confused. There is a big difference between "I feel frustrated because I have to wait" and "He is unprofessional."[6] Becoming aware of our feelings and learning to express them appropriately is thus a very important step in developing intercultural competence.

Recognizing the whole spectrum of feelings is important because it gives us a much more multifaceted understanding of our stories and situations. We all have positive and negative feelings throughout the day, sometimes simultaneously. We may be excited and proud because of our promotion but at the same time feel anxious about the new responsibilities we will have and sad about leaving our colleagues behind. Table 7.1 provides a selective list of feelings, adapted from an "inventory" compiled by the Center for Nonviolent Communication[7] as a resource for facilitating self-discovery and understanding between people.

Thoughts, Feelings, and Actions

Emotions are an essential part of being human. *Emotions* are instinctive, innate physiological reactions triggered by perceived or recalled conditions in the external environment. Universal emotions include fear, anger, sadness, joy, and disgust. Feelings, on the other hand, are mental experiences of body states.[8] While basic emotions are universal, feelings are personal and heavily influenced by culture. *Feelings* reflect assumptions and values about what is good or bad. Feelings are the result of our interpretations, or the stories we tell ourselves about the experiences we have.[9] If you hear a noise outside your bedroom and start telling yourself that someone is about to break in and kill you, your heart will start pounding and you will be inundated with a sense of fear. However, if you

Table 7.1 List of feeling words

Affectionate	Compassionate, friendly, loving, open hearted, sympathetic, tender, warm
Confident	Empowered, open, proud, safe, secure
Engaged	Absorbed, alert, curious, engrossed, fascinated, interested, intrigued, involved, stimulated
Hopeful	Expectant, encouraged, optimistic
Excited	Amazed, animated, ardent, aroused, astonished, dazzled, eager, energetic, enthusiastic, giddy, invigorated, lively, passionate, surprised, vibrant
Grateful	Appreciative, moved, thankful, touched
Inspired	Amazed, awed, wonder
Joyful	Amused, delighted, glad, happy, jubilant, pleased, tickled
Exhilarated	Blissful, ecstatic, elated, enthralled, exuberant, radiant, rapturous, thrilled
Peaceful	Calm, clear-headed, comfortable, centered, content, equanimous, fulfilled, mellow, quiet, relaxed, relieved, satisfied, serene, still, tranquil, trusting
Refreshed	Enlivened, rejuvenated, renewed, rested, restored, revived
Afraid	Apprehensive, frightened, mistrustful, panicked, scared, suspicious, terrified, wary, worried
Annoyed	Aggravated, dismayed, disgruntled, displeased, exasperated, frustrated, impatient, irritated, irked
Angry	Enraged, furious, incensed, indignant, irate, livid, outraged, resentful
Aversion	Animosity, appalled, contempt, disgusted, dislike, hate, horrified, hostile, repulsed
Confused	Ambivalent, baffled, bewildered, dazed, hesitant, lost, mystified, perplexed, puzzled, torn
Disconnected	Alienated, aloof, apathetic, bored, cold, detached, distant, distracted, indifferent, numb, removed, uninterested, withdrawn
Disquiet	Agitated, alarmed, discombobulated, disconcerted, disturbed, perturbed, rattled, restless, shocked, startled, surprised, troubled, turbulent, turmoil, uncomfortable, uneasy, unnerved, unsettled, upset
Embarrassed	Ashamed, chagrined, flustered, guilty, mortified, self-conscious

Fatigue	Beat, burnt out, depleted, exhausted, lethargic, listless, sleepy, tired, weary, worn out
Pain	Agony, anguished, bereaved, devastated, grief, heartbroken, hurt, lonely, miserable, regretful, remorseful
Sad	Depressed, dejected, despair, despondent, disappointed, discouraged, disheartened, forlorn, gloomy, heavy-hearted, hopeless, melancholy, unhappy, wretched
Tense	Anxious, cranky, distressed, distraught, edgy, fidgety, frazzled, irritable, jittery, nervous, overwhelmed, restless, stressed out
Vulnerable	Fragile, guarded, helpless, insecure, leery, reserved, sensitive, shaky
Yearning	Envious, jealous, longing, nostalgic, pining, wistful

hear the same noise and think your neighbor is out doing something in her backyard, you turn over and go back to sleep. And, if you think your partner has arrived home, you feel joy and excitement. The noise has not changed, but your story has. Figure 7.1 illustrates this process.

As we experience an unfamiliar or unexpected behavior, we attempt to make sense of it by constructing a story that will help us understand what is happening, why it is happening, how we are supposed to feel about it, and what would be the most logical next step. Our stories will elicit feelings, which will influence how we act. Given how different our stories may be in intercultural interactions, it is no surprise that strong feelings may arise.

Understanding the link between our stories, feelings, and actions is critical. If we are not able to manage our feelings, our actions may not be the most efficient or appropriate. For example, you are in a meeting and you notice that your colleague is constantly interrupting you. You may create a story in your mind that your colleague does not value your ideas and is trying to show the boss that he is in charge. You then feel betrayed and angry and make demeaning comments against your colleague. Alternatively, you can think that your colleague is really excited and can't contain his passion for the project, and you gently steer the conversation so your opinion can

Figure 7.1 Thoughts, emotions, and actions

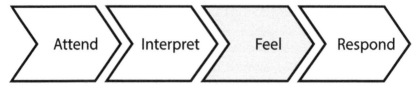

be heard. Feelings do not just happen; they are a product of the way we think about the experiences we have. If you assume there is one right away to communicate, you feel entitled to be angry with those who do not comply. However, if your story is one of curiosity and appreciation for differences, instead of anger you may feel empathy or interest.

Not all emotions come from explicit thoughts. Some feelings are reactions to submerged memories, things that happened in the past and are now buried below our level of awareness. These may include impressions about people of a cultural or ethnic group that escape our intellectual understanding. These subconscious feelings may have significant implications for how we interact with people from other cultures and may impede the development of our intercultural competence. Let me share a personal example. When I was six years old I broke my arm and needed to undergo a painful process of physiotherapy for my recovery. My physiotherapist was a stern German woman, very competent but, to my six-year-old eyes, tough and cold. Those treatment sessions were extremely painful, and I did not enjoy them. I came to associate my pain with my physiotherapist ("She hurts me") and disliked her deeply. Much later in life I realized I did not feel comfortable with people who had the same phenotype. I had absolutely no rational reason to dislike them and did not have explicit stereotypes that could justify my discomfort. Upon reflection, I realized that my discomfort came from the painful association I had imprinted in my memory as a child and did not belong in my current experience. This example highlights the fact that gut feelings and intuition often come from memories or observations below the level of awareness and are not always warranted.

Taking the time to probe into these feelings is critical for the development of intercultural competence. Instead of acting on them (by avoiding people of a certain ethnic or cultural background), we *need to be curious and investigate where our feelings are coming from and which stories are feeding them.* As you experience feelings about various cultural groups, consider whether they come from a past experience, a story, the media, or something else. Consider whether those feelings have a place in your current experience and whether they help you create understanding.

Culture and Feelings

Through our upbringing, we learn which feelings are okay to express and which are not. In some cultures – and households – anger is acceptable, but sadness is not. In others, it is okay to express negative emotions but not affection or gratitude. And in others, emotions are better not expressed at all. For example, several studies document the differences in emotion display between East Asians and Americans. Compared to Americans, East Asians tend to seek a balance between negative and positive emotions while Americans tend to resolve contradictions and polarize attitudes (positive or negative). Further, the American cultural script tends to emphasize the maximization of positive emotions,[10] and Americans are often perceived as (perhaps excessively) cheerful by other cultures[11] ("This is *fantastic!*").

As we master rules associated with emotional expression we also learn to use emotional displays as tools to get things in the world. We learn to control our emotions and display the appropriate emotions on different occasions even if they are not true to what we feel (we know we are supposed to look sad at a funeral and joyous at a wedding). We learn to theatrically[12] manipulate our displays of emotion and engage in emotional work to our personal benefit. People working in jobs that require a specific emotional outlook become skilled at expressing emotions that may not necessarily be aligned with their feelings. For example, a salesperson may learn to display positive emotions to sell more; teachers may seem enthusiastic about a topic they find tedious; and social workers may learn to show empathy and equanimity in all sorts of situations they may regard with anger, disgust, or sadness. As a result of this process of suppressing the expression of emotions to comply with societal, organizational, or professional rules of cultural expression, some of us may find it difficult to recognize and name the feelings that arise.

Within a monocultural environment our difficulties in naming emotions may not necessarily pose a problem, as we are able to communicate how we feel without recognizing and naming these feelings, just by following cultural scripts. José, a Venezuelan educated in Canada, reflected on his experience of working in Venezuela and facing the nerve-wracking news that his new employer might be closing shop and that he might lose his job: "Venezuelans tend to make everything a joke … [My life became] a daily stand-up comedy to survive the crisis and again boost my motivation." When José felt distressed and anxious about the possibility of losing his job, he recognized that an acceptable way to display this emotional distress in the Venezuelan environment was through joking about it. By doing that, he found support among his other colleagues who were facing the same distressing situation.

However, in a different cultural environment the same behavior could potentially not have the desired results, and José's use of humor to deal with a company crisis could be seen as inappropriate. That is what happened to Rosario, a Spanish woman who was sent on a work assignment to the company's subsidiary in Germany. In her first day at the German subsidiary, upon receiving a phone call informing her that her beloved grandmother had passed away, she burst into tears at her desk. She was appalled that her German colleagues did not come to talk to her or provide comfort. Her German colleagues did not know how to react to her outburst and thought it was not professional behavior. As we engage in intercultural situations where our learned display of emotions does not fit the norm, we need to get in touch with our feelings to express them appropriately.

Stop for a moment and consider what you have learnt about expressing emotions. Which feelings are you free to express and which emotions are better kept in hiding? How did you learn that? Through your family, or professional training, or general societal influences?

Working with Our Feelings

Labeling feelings is a powerful tool we can use to manage them. Brain research suggests that when we are able to find words to describe our feelings we deactivate the part of the brain that initiates a stress response.[13] For example, psychology scholar David Creswell and his colleagues used functional magnetic resonance imaging (fMRI) to explore the role of labeling emotions in calming the brain. In an experiment, participants were shown photographs of people who were emotionally upset. In one group, they were asked to label the expressed emotion (e.g., anger, fear), and in the control group they were asked to match the person's gender with a corresponding name (e.g., Peter or Susan). They found that the amygdala – the part of the brain that sounds an alarm in times of danger – was less active in the group tasked with labeling emotions.[14] For this reason, dialogue with a professional is at the core of many therapeutic treatments. As we speak about our feelings, we find ways to express our emotions and through this process construct new meanings and perspectives.[15]

In the context of adjustment to foreign environments, research suggests that venting in supportive face-to-face communication helps individuals to shift perspectives and enhances control.[16] When we express our feelings to a sympathetic listener, we are able to articulate our problems and feelings in ways that help us to be more objective and resolve our issues. That is, as we tell one another our stories, we are able to reconstruct them and find ways to solve the problems they represent. (A note of caution: the sympathetic listener is *not* the person with whom we are having the intercultural interaction, but a trusted friend, coach, mentor, or therapist.) We may vent to an independent listener in order to make sense of our feelings, feel better, and prepare for our "difficult" interactions. When we are communicating about an emotionally charged issue, it is important to express our feelings carefully. In other words, it may be that you need to vent to feel better, but the venting should be something you do outside of the interaction – before, after, or in between encounters.

In the absence of a sympathetic listener, reflective journaling can help us manage our feelings and facilitate the development of intercultural competence by increasing emotional comfort and giving us a sense of control. Through written journaling, we are able to simulate the benefits of ventilation and, in the absence of a sounding board, become our own sympathetic companions. As writer Julia Cameron suggests, through reflective writing "we witness ourselves ... writing gives us a place to say what we need to say, but also hear what we need to hear."[17] Reflective journaling can help us deal with feelings of loneliness, confusion, and culture shock and enable us to develop ways of coping with new surroundings by providing us with the space to focus inward, enabling us to become aware of and honor our thoughts and feelings. Reflections are particularly important for managing our feelings when we are out of our element, such as when we are immersed in an unfamiliar culture when traveling, moving, or joining a new community group and are facing a disruption in our support network.

A note of caution, though: when we are experiencing or reflecting upon negative feelings, we may try to counter them in unconstructive ways, appeasing our anxieties through defense mechanisms, as opposed to learning from them. It is important to control this defensive instinct, and focus on accepting the negative feelings and attempting to understand their causes. If I am upset because I feel pushed into a corner by my business partner, rather than trying to resolve my frustration by blaming and judging, I need to look deeper to see what is underneath – such as feelings of lack of control and lack of appreciation.

Venting and journaling are good tools for making sense of our feelings and reconsidering the stories we are telling ourselves when we are able to step back from an interaction. However, it is not always possible to pause and regroup. When we are in the heat of an argument or emotionally charged situation, we need to find ways to manage our feelings on the spot. By intentionally focusing attention on our thoughts and feelings, we can avoid "knee-jerk" reactions and create an opportunity to respond to stress in different and better ways.

The process of focusing inward on our thoughts and feelings is commonly referred to as *mindfulness practice*, and is often recommended by psychologists to help patients deal with stress and alleviate mental and physical tension. Mindfulness practice draws on Buddhist thinking and consists of intentionally and non-judgmentally focusing on the "here and now," paying attention to what is happening with our body and mind.[18]

Stop for a moment. Take a deep breath and mentally scan your body. Are there any tensions? Starting with your feet, move your attention up your body, checking each body part for comfort. Perhaps your posture needs to be adjusted. Perhaps there is tension in your legs, back, or neck. Try to relax any tense areas and move your body gently to find a more comfortable position. Now focus on your feelings. How are you feeling right now? Notice any thoughts or feelings that emerge. Do not judge or attempt to solve them. Just notice what is happening with you right now and let it be. Take a few breaths before continuing.

Managing feelings means being able to express our feelings carefully and calmly.[19] There is a difference between calmly stating, "This situation is making me frustrated" and stomping in frustration. Often, feelings are an important part of the problem and they need to be expressed. For example, you may be discussing a project deadline that makes you uncomfortable because you feel it creates too much pressure and anxiety. You need to express your concerns about the deadline, but your anxiety and stress are an important part of the problem and need to be expressed as well. Communication scholar Douglas Stone and colleagues further suggest that when expressing feelings, we need to express the full spectrum of them.[20] That is, we seldom feel just one thing. You may be anxious about the project deadline but at the same time feel excited about the project, honored to be part of the team, conflicted about letting go of other priorities, hopeful for the outcome of the project, and so on. When expressing the full spectrum of feelings, we bring more depth to the conversation and provide others with the opportunity to better understand our perspectives.

Sometimes you may decide that expressing your feelings is not helpful. For example, it may be that the problem and the feelings are really about what is going on inside you and are not the result of the other person's behavior. For example, if your personal history has caused you to dislike a particular group of people and feel disgust about certain types of behavior, expressing your feelings of disgust may not help build a more cooperative interaction. Rather, you need a *conversation with yourself* to reflect upon your own assumptions about what is right and wrong and your inability to deal with the situation calmly and openly.

Managing feelings is about more than noticing and avoiding negativity; it is also about fostering positivity. Positivity has been found to broaden the mind and increase attentiveness, increase creativity, provide a new outlook on life, and change the way we interact with the world. The more positive we feel, the more open we are to finding new solutions and trusting others. Positive psychology scholar Barbara Fredrickson suggests that the following ten positive feelings are particularly important in everyday life: joy, gratitude, serenity, interest, hope, pride, amusement, inspiration, awe, and love.[21]

Positive psychology is a relatively new area of research within psychology, focusing on helping people flourish as opposed to alleviating suffering. From these new advances, we learn the importance of finding the positive in our situations – that is, seeing the glass as half full rather than half empty. Emerging research in cross-cultural and intercultural studies suggests that we will benefit from looking at the positive outcomes of cultural diversity as opposed to the challenges and conflicts that may result from differences in cultural background. In intercultural situations, we may treasure our common humanity, be grateful for the opportunity to learn new things, and connect with different people.

Developing Empathy

Intercultural interactions are a two-way street. Not only must we be concerned with how we are feeling, we also need to attempt to understand how the other is feeling. *Empathy* refers to the ability to identify and understand others' feelings and motives. It is a shift in perspective, from seeing others from the outside to putting ourselves into their shoes – trying to look at the world through their eyes. If we are grappling with intense feelings and threats to our sense of self, so is our counterpart. Empathy helps us see the other in a new light.

Developing empathy starts with talking yourself into being curious and seeking to understand other people, rather than rejecting their views. That may not be easy. We are often tempted to assume that we already understand how the other person feels or thinks. However, there is always more to learn and understand. Empathy requires acknowledging the complexity and contradictions that make up our lives. Often, there are aspects of the other person's story that we do not fully understand and that, if we did, would change the way we feel about them, their views, and how we interact with them.

One of the main challenges in being empathetic is that it is threatening to question our own assumptions – what if I have been wrong all along? When we are faced with people whose points of view we do not agree with, we often react defensively, thinking that the only possible explanation for the difference is that they do not know what we know (as opposed to thinking that we may not know what they know). We may think ,"If they were better informed, more civilized, more educated, they of course would think like I do." We need to be aware of such reactions, which are barriers to understanding. Empathy requires opening up to the possibility that a different view is not wrong or misinformed, just a different way to make sense of reality. The point here is to accept and understand that the people in front of us are complex cultural beings and that their actions and views make sense within their cultural framework and the stories that make up their life. It is very arrogant of us to think that we are right and millions of people are wrong when we don't understand something. Ask yourself: "What else do I need to know for this story to make more sense to me? How I can understand the world in such a way that this behavior would make sense?" Empathy can help us all to foster understanding and decrease the negative impacts of the divisive rhetoric gaining popularity nowadays.

Just like us, people who don't share our views may find it equally difficult to question their assumptions and may get defensive when faced with opinions with which they disagree. Using rational arguments alone to convince them that they are wrong and we are right is not likely to work unless we understand and acknowledge the feelings and identity issues that are involved. If adopting your point of view means that they will feel less competent, valued, or worthy, chances are they will get defensive and resist your ideas. If the conversation goes toward the direction of who is right, both sides are likely to stick to their positions and defend their points of view. Changing our view on a topic is an emotional process with important implications for the way we feel and think about ourselves.

While empathy is a goal worth striving toward, the reality is that we will never fully understand the other, as we are multifaceted, contradictory, cultural beings. Empathy in intercultural situations may arise less from shared values, assumptions, and experiences (e.g., I know how that feels) than from the common fact that we are complex cultural beings and our thoughts, feelings, and behaviors are influenced by cultural and contextual forces outside our awareness. In this case, *trying* to understand the other may be all that is needed. Psychologists suggest that we are more interested in knowing that others are trying to be empathetic than in believing that they have actually achieved the goal of understanding us.[22]

The Road Ahead

Intercultural interactions may elicit strong feelings. We need to be mindful of those feelings, as they influence not only how we see situations but also how others see them. We must acknowledge that our differing views cannot always be reconciled by rational arguments alone, and that we need to be sensitive to the feelings that lie behind them. To create the conditions for collaboration, we need to step out of our own stories and together construct a *neutral story* that includes how we feel about the issues at hand and preserves how we feel about ourselves. This requires strong communication skills, which are discussed in the next chapter.

Reflective Exercise

This exercise invites you to observe your emotional landscape and the way your feelings and thoughts are interconnected. Consider an emotional situation you are currently facing. It could be a project generating anxiety, feelings toward another person, or anticipation of your vacation travel.

Tell Your Story
Write a detailed description of an intercultural situation. Draw on all your senses and make your description as rich and detailed as

possible. What was the context of this situation? Who was there? What was influencing your behavior? What did you say or do? What did others say or do? How were you feeling?

Which dominant feelings are associated with this situation? Which other feelings were/are present that may have been overlooked? Using the list of feeling words in table 7.1 identify the feelings that were/are present for you and others.

Revisit Your Story

Leave your story aside for at least one hour. Then, revisit your story by asking yourself the following questions:

- ✓ Are there facts, thoughts, or details not considered in your description that could change your interpretation of the story?
- ✓ What assumptions were guiding your actions? What knowledge might have influenced you?
- ✓ When interacting with others, what were you trying to achieve? Did you respond effectively? What were the consequences of your actions for others and yourself? What would be the consequences had you responded differently? What factors might prevent you from responding in new ways?
- ✓ How did you feel and why did you feel that way? How did your feelings influence your actions? What were others' feelings and why did they feel that way? How do you feel about this experience now?
- ✓ How does this situation connect with other experiences?
- • To what extent have your feelings constrained your ability to respond effectively?
- • To what extent have you demonstrated empathy toward the other?
- • How can this situation be reframed to elicit positive emotions? What is (was) good or right about this situation? What are you grateful for? How would a more positive outlook allow you to respond differently?

Prepare for the Future and Apply Learning
- ✓ What insights have you gained from this experience, and what are their implications for the future?

✓ Does this situation require further action? Of what kind? Are there things you need to say or do? Are there knowledge gaps you need to cover? How can you validate your conclusions?

✓ Based on what you have learned, how are you approaching new situations?

• In preparing for the future, consider how you can better manage your feelings. What tools or resources can you use to increase your emotional literacy?

• In preparing for the future, consider how you can increase your levels of empathy for others.

Key Points

• Intercultural interactions have the potential to elicit strong positive and negative feelings. While positive feelings support our interactions by broadening our mind and facilitating cooperation, negative feelings hinder our ability to be open and receptive to new ideas and points of view.

• Intercultural interactions may elicit feelings of uncertainty, ambiguity, and anxiety. We experience *uncertainty* when we are unable to predict or explain the behavior of others. We experience *ambiguity* when we are unable to make sense of or interpret facts and situations. We experience *anxiety* when we are uneasy or apprehensive about what will happen when we interact with people from other cultures.

• A prerequisite for the development of intercultural competence is the ability to recognize, acknowledge, and process feelings. That includes noticing subtle contradictory feelings and preventing them from being transformed into judgments, attributions, characterizations, and conclusions.

• Our cultural upbringing influences our perceptions of which feelings are okay for us to express and which are not. For this reason, learning to articulate our feelings, as opposed to naturally expressing them, is critical for the development of intercultural competence.

- Working with our feelings starts with labeling them and then re-examining the stories we tell ourselves that make us feel the way we do.
- Dialogue therapy, venting, journaling, and mindfulness practice are useful tools for increasing our emotional awareness and developing strategies for coping with our feelings.
- Empathy refers to the ability to identify and understand *others'* feelings and motives and find better ways to work with them. Empathy facilitates understanding by helping us see the other in a new light.

CHAPTER 8

Communicating across Cultures

The most important thing in communication is hearing what isn't said.

Peter Drucker

Communication is the essence of intercultural interactions. It is through communication that we exchange ideas; develop and dissolve relationships; and negotiate understanding, behavior, and tangible outcomes. Communication also makes cultural differences salient and can be a catalyst for both synergy and conflict. Despite the prevalence of communication in our everyday life, effective communication is a challenging task even within cultural groups. We all have experienced difficult conversations when we need to express frustrations or come to agreement regarding issues that are emotionally charged.[1] When communicating across cultures, we may find that even simple interactions can become problematic, and different assumptions can easily lead to confusion and misunderstanding. People may have different understandings about when things are supposed to be done; important pieces of information may not be heard; comments that were intended to be harmless may be taken as personal attacks, and so on. This chapter explores the ways in which culture influences communication and discusses mechanisms we can use to communicate more effectively in intercultural situations. It starts with a look at how culture provides us with the common ground required to facilitate communication.

Culture and Common Ground

A community's culture provides members with the *common ground* required to go about their everyday life. Common ground consists of mutually *known* – even if not uniformly agreed on – knowledge, beliefs, and assumptions about what is acceptable or not acceptable, desirable or undesirable.[2] In other words, having common ground makes it easier to deal with people from our own culture not necessarily because we *agree* on what is good or bad, right or wrong, but because we know what to expect from each other. In the words of interculturalist Joseph Shaules, "the mark of shared cultural knowledge is not the degree to which our behavior is typical or non-typical; it is the degree to which we are capable of successfully interpreting behavior in accordance with community standards."[3] For example, a Brazilian person may not like soccer, but she expects and accepts that there will be soccer conversations in the office after an important match, and she can predict the mood of her colleagues based on the results of the match. She also knows the expected protocols around soccer conversations – that is, she knows what to say and what not to say when a soccer conversation is taking place. *Cultural competence* is manifested by our ability to interpret others' behavior and predict how they will interpret our behavior rather than by our agreement with the values or assumptions of a cultural community.

Common ground facilitates communication between individuals of the same culture and makes everyday interactions more efficient. A common culture provides people with implicit parameters that shape interaction between members, making communication easier by helping people fill in the gaps left by what is unsaid.[4] In our own cultural communities, we may choose to deviate from norms of conduct to make a statement. For example, you may know both that you are expected to engage in "small talk" at the beginning of a work meeting and what topics it is appropriate to discuss, but you may *choose* to stay quiet because you want to show your coworkers your dissatisfaction with a decision they have made. This non-conforming behavior is different from the behavior of a naive foreigner who is unaware that small talk is expected.

Common ground is created through participation in a common community (e.g., we are both Italians, we both work in the same organization, we are both physicians, we are both scuba divers); through shared experience (e.g., we both worked together on this report); or through personal exchanges (e.g., you told me about an experience you had). All our interactions rely on the common ground we have built with our counterpart. The more we get to know another person, the more common ground we are able to develop. The more we interact with someone, the less relevant his or her cultural background becomes. As we get to know our coworker or business partner, we rely on our own individualized common ground to communicate. We no longer need to rely on general rules (e.g., Mexicans are polychronic and see time as flexible) but can rely on our shared understanding about each other and how we do things together (when I work with Carlos, I expect that he will come to meetings right on time, but Ana tends to be late).

The need to develop common ground explains why it takes longer for multicultural than for monocultural teams to develop the trust and work processes required to work efficiently. Multicultural teams first need to develop common ground, which is accomplished much faster when we are working with people who have grown up in similar communities, have had a similar education, and share similar life experiences. The need for a common set of assumptions and knowledge that we share and can rely on suggests that we need to either *make assumptions about what is mutually known* – and risk being wrong – or *take the time to establish mutual understanding through communication*. Figure 8.1 illustrates the role of communication in creating common ground. Through communication we make thoughts and feelings known to the other person and establish

Figure 8.1 Communication and common ground

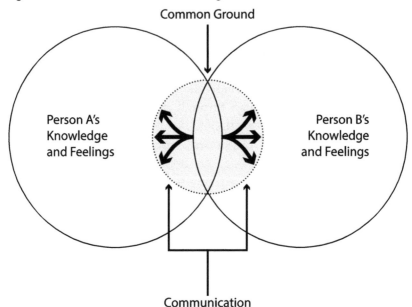

common ground (gray circle). Communication mechanisms used to create common ground will be discussed later in this chapter.

Stop for a second and consider the very last interaction you had before reading this. It may have been a short sentence to your partner letting her know you were going to do some reading, or it may have been a quick comment at the bus station. Whatever it was, think of the most recent sentence you have spoken (e-mailed or texted). Now consider all the knowledge that is required for another person to understand what you meant. Imagine that someone from a different culture and context got hold of your communication and is trying to understand your sentence. Assuming that language is not an issue, could that person understand what you meant? Most likely you relied on quite a lot of common ground – knowledge of shared knowledge – to make your communication as efficient as possible. My latest message was to my husband – a text message that said only, "at the roundabout." To decide on that message, I relied on our common knowledge that I was going to meet him at his workplace, and that there is a roundabout close to his building where it is possible to stop the car without blocking the traffic, and that with that simple three-word message he would know what to do – come out of the building and walk toward the car.

Communication involves interacting within a social and physical context to arrive at an understanding of what is going on in order to act based on this understanding. As discussed in chapter 3, this process is cyclical and happens through communication. As we communicate, we focus our attention on a set of words, body language, facial expressions, and surrounding circumstances; interpret these disparate bits of information as a message; decide how we feel about it; and then construct a message in response (action).[5] As we respond, we create an experience for the other person, who, in turn, will need to attend, interpret, feel, and respond.

Our communication process is filtered by our *cultural lenses*,[6] as culture influences the process of attending, interpreting, feeling, and responding. For example, comparative research suggests that Americans – who are raised in an individualistic society – are more likely to rely on the isolated properties of people or objects they are examining to attach meaning or enhance understanding. As a result, when they see an individual, they tend to mentally classify him or her as male or female, black or white, professional or blue-collar, and so forth. On the other hand, Chinese – who are raised in a more collectivist environment – tend to classify people based on criteria that emphasize relationships and contexts. As a result, they are more likely to first see someone as a member of a group, clan, or organization, instead of focusing on the person's individual characteristics. The same difference in categorization processes can be found in many other domains, influencing how we make sense of a message.

Culture also provides us with *communication protocols*, or behaviors, that may influence how we communicate and how we expect others to communicate. Communication protocols include what is considered an appropriate topic for discussion, such as people's willingness to discuss personal matters, family, politics, religion, or money. For example, a French blogger has discussed differences in protocols around money as follows: "While people [in North America] don't obsess with money, it is perfectly acceptable to talk about finances, debts, and to pass on money-related tips ... I got used to talking about money now. I just hope I don't embarrass my French friends too much ..."[7] Communication protocols also include other conversational formalities, such as the appropriateness of getting down to business without warming up with broad or general discussions. It may also include the degree of formality expected in a conversation and the degree to which apologies or notes of appreciation are called for.

Culture often places constraints and expectations on what is considered acceptable communication behavior. For example, in the United States people are often expected and encouraged to be assertive and to take the initiative in conversations. By contrast, in much of Asia, people are often expected to remain silent and wait for an invitation to speak. While in North America it is acceptable to leave a conversation once the main topic is finished, in Spain people are generally expected to linger awhile and talk about other things before departing. These differences may be prevalent even in countries that are culturally close, like the United States and Canada. An American blogger discussed his experience in communicating with Canadians as follows: "Canadians are much quieter, more reticent, and they don't like to talk about themselves; it clearly makes them uncomfortable ... But where Canadians don't talk much, they have a very intricate and subtle body language ... It was a bit unnerving when I went for a job interview last spring and there was a group of people sitting around the table, conducting the interview. The eyes were flashing all around the table and the subtle twitching was going on, but no one was saying anything. It was spooky. I wasn't sure if I was doing alright or not." These cultural screens have the potential to create confusion and challenge our taken-for-granted assumptions about what is acceptable or unacceptable communication behavior. The American blogger concluded, "Turns out I got the job, but it made me feel like I hadn't quite made it into the group yet. I was still an immigrant, an American, an outsider."[8]

Communication is not only about the words we say. Anthropologist Edward Hall[9] points out that we communicate with each other through behavior, not just words, suggesting that cultural assumptions in general are often part of a *silent language* used to convey meaning without words. Silent communication is the use of nonverbal or visual communication (e.g., facial expressions, gestures, the use of personal space, opulent surroundings, etc.) to convey a message. Hall suggests that cultures vary in the extent to which they rely on information in the physical context or that is assumed to be internalized by participants versus explicit codes to transmit a message. While culture may influence how much we rely on contextual cues, studies suggest that, typically, verbal communication carries less than 35 percent of the meaning in a message.[10] This suggests that we need to focus not only on the content of the message but also on the accompanying nonverbal messages and contextual cues that go along with it.

Take a moment to reflect on your communication style. Think about your assumptions about what is an appropriate topic for discussion. How do you feel about discussing your income, your personal life, or your views on religion or politics? What topics are you comfortable discussing with a complete stranger? Consider the behaviors that are typical in a conversation within your cultural group. Consider how you may alter your communication behavior when you talk with different people.

Estimating Common Ground

Anytime we interact with someone we do not know well, we need to estimate our common ground, or make inferences about the assumptions, beliefs, and knowledge that are shared and that have a bearing in the current situation. (Note that differences in assumptions and knowledge may happen any time people from different cultural communities interact and do not occur only when individuals come from different countries.) Succeeding in intercultural interactions requires the ability to recognize the absence of common ground and to create common ground by explaining to others how we think and behave as well as by inquiring about others' thoughts and behaviors. Psycholinguistic scholar Herbert Clark referred to the process of achieving understanding about what is commonly known and assumed as *grounding*.[11]

Grounding is the collective process by which individuals try to achieve the mutual belief that they have reached a level of understanding that is *sufficient for current purposes*. Grounding is highly dependent on current purposes: we need a lot less common ground for engaging in a short sales transaction than for developing a new product together. Individuals may share significant knowledge and understanding but must establish – for current purposes – which aspects of their common ground are relevant.

When we make sense of a situation, we combine pieces of information into coherent stories. We create our stories by ordering and connecting facts, observations, and assumptions and mentally filling in the gaps left by what was not said. We rely on our previous knowledge and interpretation schemas to make sense of new situations and make inferences about other people's behavior. In intercultural situations, these interpretation schemas and this previous knowledge may be inappropriate and need to be revised. Through interaction with others we are able to come up with a common understanding of what is going on and what we need to do next. The first step in this process is to estimate our common ground – what knowledge and assumptions do we share? Consider the simple communication interaction below, which I experienced in my hometown as I was going about my everyday life.

– "When will my car be ready?" I asked the Somali man in charge of the car wash.

– "It takes about two to three hours," he said.

– "So, if I come back at three p.m., will it be ready?" I tried to confirm (it was noon).

– "Come later. We are open until seven p.m."

– "I have to pick up my son at school at five p.m. not far from here." I said, trying to get a firmer answer.

– "If your car is not ready at five p.m., you can borrow my car," he answered.

– "Ok, thanks. My husband will pick up the car later in the evening."

This short communication exchange has many layers of cultural assumptions and, to someone distracted, can quickly lead to frustrations. My husband arrived at the car shop at 5:30 and the car was only "almost ready." Had I assumed that the car would be ready for picking up my son and getting to various places on time, I would have had a rather stressful evening. Through our interaction, we attempted to establish enough understanding regarding when the car would be ready. Notice that the process of grounding was facilitated by my attempts to confirm my understanding of his communication.

When the service person told me, "It takes about two to three hours," I could have stopped the conversation and left the shop. However, since I did not know him, and I know people may have different understandings about time, I attempted to confirm my understanding that the car would be ready at three p.m. by asking, "So, if I come back at three p.m. will it be ready?" His answer, "Come later. We are open until seven p.m.," suggested to me that our understanding of three hours was not the same and that he was not able to guarantee that the car would be ready at three p.m. At this point, I realized I needed to get more information to reach common ground. So, I told him what my constraints were, "I have to pick up my son at school at five p.m. not far from here." Through this sentence, I made clear to him what my situation was. His answer was, "If your car is not ready at five, you can borrow my car." Here he acknowledged that he understood my predicament but still could not guarantee that the car would be ready on time. I then decided I did not want to risk being in a difficult situation and decided to make alternative arrangements. We thus reached a common understanding that the car might not be ready by five p.m. and that the car would be picked up later in the evening.

This exchange is not necessarily a reflection of the cultures involved but a process to create understanding when it is not clear that communication rules are shared. Note that many possible alternative scenarios are possible here: I could have told him, for example, that if he could not guarantee that the car would be ready by five p.m. I would not leave the car there. What is important is not who is right or wrong but that the two of us needed to come to a common understanding of what to do next – or risk being disappointed.

Cultural self-awareness (discussed in chapter 4) is a building block for estimating common ground. Awareness of our own values, beliefs, styles, and patterns of behavior can help us identify when a thought, assumption, or preference may not be shared. This awareness may prompt us to explain or inquire about things we would normally take for granted in a monocultural situation. Even though we may not know what others know and share with us, we know that our knowledge and assumptions are culture-specific, and we can quickly recognize when common ground is missing. When scheduling a meeting, for example, we need to recognize that the other person may not share our knowledge and assumptions about time and quickly explain what we mean.

When communicating, we need to be aware of the interpretational leaps we are making and the assumptions we are using to fill in the gaps of what is not said. As we communicate with others it is important to *separate facts from interpretations*. For example, your counterpart arrived at 9:15 to a meeting that was scheduled for 9:00. The fact is "the meeting was scheduled for 9:00 and he arrived at 9:15." The interpretation of what that means may vary from "He was reasonably on time" to "He was terribly late." The implications of these interpretations are even more subjective and may vary from "He is unreliable," or "He does not value our relationship," to "Something must have come up." In intercultural interactions, we must be aware of the interpretational leaps we make based on facts and must *come back to the facts* again and again and inquire whether there are other possible interpretations. "She asked me how much money I make" is a fact. "She is nosy" is an interpretation. By focusing on facts, we let go of our implicit assumptions and interpretations and focus on communicating the facts we see to arrive at a common understanding *together*.

How we interpret things has profound implications for how we relate to others. We tend to attribute intentions to others based on our assumptions of common ground. A person who does not engage in small talk at the beginning of a meeting may be *assumed* to have an intention of rudeness. In such cases, it is important to probe the stories we are telling ourselves and separate the facts (or actions we observed) from our interpretation, the impact the behavior has on us, and the assumptions we are making.[12] We may start by considering, "What did the person do?" She arrived at 9:15 for a meeting scheduled for 9:00. Then we need to take ownership of our reactions to what the person did. *"What was the impact on me?"* The impact was that I felt unappreciated. *"What assumptions am I making?"* I am assuming she does not value me. Once we recognize that we are making an interpretation based on an assumption that may not be shared, we need to bring as much information to the table as possible to create common ground.

In intercultural interactions, we often do not have the same knowledge, beliefs, or points of view. Thus, assembling a common understanding, or story, of what is happening requires an attitude of openness and curiosity. The starting point of this conversation is not who is right or wrong but rather *"Why do we see things differently?"* We may inquire about knowledge, facts, and reasons to better understand the other side's point of view. We need to understand their story, to see how their conclusions make sense within it, and to help them understand the story in which our conclusions make sense.[13]

Creating Common Ground

Communication in intercultural situations is the main mechanism for learning about each other's points of view, knowledge, and needs. When we are communicating across cultures, the more we are able to absorb, the better we are able to understand what the other person is communicating. Thus, *listening* is a key component of effective communication. When we are communicating with people with an accent different from ours and who use words and body language in ways we do not understand, we may get side-tracked into analyzing, judging, or wondering about the speaker's delivery style and disconnect from the main message. Even when the delivery style feels comfortable, we may feel that the content of the message is not important or reasonable and may be caught thinking that the other person "does not make sense" and focus instead on our own ideas and on planning our own response in-stead of really listening and trying to capture the whole message being communicated. When listening across cultures, it is impor-tant to get past what we see as inadequacies or oddities in the way the message is delivered and to concentrate on the content of what is being communicated through words, body language, and facial expressions. Once we listen to others carefully, we may find there are still things we do not understand because of lack of common ground. To that end, inquiry and advocacy are helpful tools for expanding shared knowledge.

Inquiry[14]

Inquiry is a process of seeking new information to better understand the points of view of others. Inquiry refers to exploring and question-ing our own reasoning and the reasoning of others to understand their interpretations. While we may agree on the facts (e.g., what time people came to the meeting), we may not be clear about how we are interpreting these facts and how these interpretations influence how we feel. Inquiry is important for several reasons: first, it facilitates the exchange of information that is not shared. Even though two people may be experiencing the same situation, they may have different in-formation about it that influences their interpretations. For example, imagine that you were sent abroad by headquarters to help a subsid-iary implement a new performance evaluation process. While discussing issues in the meeting, you might not know that a similar implementation attempt had failed in the past because the local union was against the system, so that you do not understand the locals' resistance to your suggestions.

Second, when faced with the same information, different people may pay attention to different aspects of it. What becomes salient to *us* is not necessarily the most important part of an interaction but rather what *we consider* the most important part of an interaction. For example, in attempting to implement the new evaluation system you may be focused on the transparency afforded by clear evaluation processes, but your counterparts may be more concerned with the impacts on motivation.

Third, we may interpret things differently. Through the cultures in which we have been immersed we learn how things work and come to attach meanings to them. We may have learned that we are not supposed to challenge our superiors even when they are misinformed, or that a lack of questioning means a lack of interest. When we send a message to another, we attach meaning to it based on our interpretations of the issue, ourselves, and the other person. When *others* receive our message, they attach meaning to it based on *their* interpretations of the issue, the message, themselves, and us. When there is no common ground, what we intended to convey with our message may get lost, and the interpretation others make may be very different from what we intended.

Inquiry is a mechanism of attempting to uncover these different assumptions and interpretations by collecting more information. The questions that require answers are as follows: How do I/you perceive the situation? What do I/you wish to achieve in this situation? Which actions am I/are you taking to achieve this goal? Inquiry requires suspending judgment, letting go of a previous understanding, and tolerating uncertainty until a new understanding can be constructed. Through inquiry we reveal hidden cultural assumptions, clearly state the "data" on which our assumptions are based, and become aware of how our and the other's cultures are shaping our perceptions, expectations, and behaviors.

In some cultural contexts inquiry may translate into asking questions directly (i.e., "How do you see this situation?"). However, in other contexts, this direct questioning may not always be appropriate. While the need to put more information on the table and understand each other is critical, how we go about it may need to be modified as we interact with different people. The purpose is the same – to create common ground – but the format may need to be adapted. For example, to an untrained Western eye the Japanese do not disagree with their bosses. But the reality is that they do send disagreeing messages in subtle and indirect ways. It is a matter of context, time, place, and mode of expression. The method of inquiry used by a Japanese person may look very different from the method used by an American. Instead of a "put your cards on the table" approach, a much more subtle and indirect method may be used to share points of view

As a result, we need to gather information in several different ways, relying on the context, body language, subtle cues, and messages. The ability to do so typically relies heavily on *observation* and *self-reflection*. The process of inquiry starts when we ask *ourselves* questions and probe for answers in multiple ways. Once we are aware of the knowledge and assumptions informing *our* view, we may gather information through various means to understand the point of view of others. Inquiry requires a genuine interest in understanding the other person's point of view until it makes sense to us and we can together come up with an acceptable solution or agreement.

Advocacy

Advocacy refers to expressing and standing up for what one thinks and desires. Advocacy involves stating clearly what we think and want and explaining the reasoning behind our point of view. Advocacy is a tool to help *other* people understand *us*. It is difficult to shift frames and get into another person's story, especially when this story is based on a different set of cultural assumptions.[15] People need help to understand us, just as we need help to understand them. Helping others see our point of view may require some work and looking for different ways to explain our views.

Advocacy is not only about stating what we want – as in, "I want everyone to do things my way" – but about explaining the reasons behind the way we think and opening up to others to explore gaps in our reasoning. The goal of advocacy is to help others see our story and perspective. Advocacy is about making our thoughts explicit not only to others but also to ourselves. We sometimes are not aware of our own thinking and assumptions. In an ill-advised attempt to be considerate we sometimes make the mistake of focusing on what the other person is thinking at the cost of really understanding what we ourselves are thinking. We start projecting what they must be thinking or feeling, which is far less challenging than looking at what we are thinking and feeling, and why. When we do our home-work and take care of our half of the bargain, we can communicate openly and non-defensively, and give the other person the opportunity to communicate as well.

When we combine inquiry with advocacy we share information about our cultural assumptions, the meanings we attach to an issue, and the reasons for our thinking. This sharing of assumptions and interpretations creates the basis for a new, mutually acceptable meaning to emerge. There is a caveat, though. We need to be mind-ful of our purposes; our goal is to achieve understanding and agree-ment to move us to the next action, *for current purposes*. We do not need to agree on or discuss all our values and beliefs in each inter-cultural interaction we have. Rather, we need to understand and agree on the few issues that are relevant to our purposes.

Inquiry and advocacy need to be used in balance.[16] If we only in-quire, we may uncover information about the other but do not pro-vide any information about ourselves. If we only advocate, we will provide information about ourselves but not get information about the other. The construction of a shared understanding requires an exchange where we not only advocate for our views but also inquire about the other's point of view. Engaging in inquiry and advocacy is challenging because it requires uncovering our own perceptions, exposing ourselves, being open to hearing others' perceptions, and being willing to give up the safety of our own previous interpreta-tions in order for a new interpretation to emerge.

Dealing with Conflicts through Communication

The first step when a conflict arises is to recognize the real source of disagreement. Recall that culture influences behavior through several mechanisms, including beliefs, norms, values, habits, and customs (chapter 4). However, different situations make each of these mechanisms more or less important, with implications for the types of intercultural conflicts we may experience and possible solutions we may adopt.

A situation that calls for norms and schemas may result in misunderstandings, as each of us comes to a different interpretation of the situation and associated issues. Misunderstandings caused by different interpretations may be solved through communication, as we inquire about others' understandings and advocate for our views. Once a common understanding is established, these situations may or may not result in a conflict, since even when we understand what the other person is saying, we may not agree. A situation that calls for personal preferences may create a *conflict of tastes and preferences*. A situation that involves a moral judgment may create a *conflict of values*. Far more often, conflicts are about *practices*, or what we agree is an acceptable course of action moving forward. These practices are often a result of differences in what we expect, the meaning we attach to behaviors, and our values and beliefs. Let's consider each of those in more detail.[17]

Conflicts about tastes and preferences: Across different cultures, fried ants, rat soup, or cooked snails can elicit very different responses, varying from delight to disgust. Facing these differences in tastes and preferences, and assuming individuals are open enough to accept that other people may prefer different things, we may simply agree to disagree (I eat my ants, you eat your snails). In this scenario, the best course of action is to *accept* differences nonjudgmentally and *avoid* conflict. However, at times it is not possible to agree to disagree, such as in a situation in which just one dish may be ordered and we all need to agree on one of the options. In this case, it is worth exploring further if fundamental values or beliefs are involved (such as religious beliefs about eating certain animals) or if there are legal constraints (such as health guidelines across different countries). In this case, a *compromise* solution may be possible (ordering a dish everybody finds acceptable).

Conflicts about values and beliefs: Conflicts about values and beliefs are harder to deal with than conflicts about tastes and preferences, but they are less common than we are led to believe. We hold multiple values, but these values are not equally prioritized at all times and sometimes conflict with one another. For example, most of us value quality of life and relationships *and* value achievement. The difference is not in what we value but in how we assign priorities to those values at a given point in time. It may be that most of the time you value achievement over relationships, but in a particular situation, perhaps because the project in question is not very important to you or because there is a family crisis, you may assign a higher value to quality of life. The conflicts we experience are not likely to be about which value is more important but about the practices that emerge from them – do we work overtime to make this project better, or do we stop at five o'clock and go home even if the project is not as good as it could be?

Agreeing on acceptable practices is considerably easier – and more beneficial – than agreeing on how important this project is compared to other things in our lives. That is, it is best to focus on negotiating an acceptable schedule for this project as opposed to arguing about how important this project is supposed to be. Whenever possible, it is best to focus on *equifinal,* as opposed to shared, values. "Equifinality" means that multiple routes exist toward a single end, and even when values and interpretations are dissimilar it is possible to arrive at similar behavioral implications.[18] In other words, what is important is that we agree on how much to work on the project, even if one person is working on this project because she values achievement while another is focused on the group's welfare and the importance of teamwork.

Conflicts about practices: Conflicts about acceptable practices are at the core of intercultural problems. Through interaction we need to come up with an agreement – for *current purposes* – of what is going on and what we need to do next. Resolving conflicts about acceptable practices requires an attitude of *humility*, which allows us to view our differences nonjudgmentally. Our differences are not right or wrong or better or worse; they are just differences.[19] Differences are not to be *tolerated* as in "They are wrong, but I will tolerate them." Rather, we need to take those different perspectives as a starting point to build understanding. It is not easy to let go of what we believe and want. It is much more comfortable to judge the other as unreasonable and stick to our ways of thinking and seeing the world. Other people's frames of reference may be too unlike ours for us to embrace them, and their points of view may be too difficult to accept. In these situations, we should not lose track of the fact that intercultural competence is not about agreeing on *values or preferences* but about agreeing on how to move forward.

Following the example of how much work to put in on the report, we need to be able to describe the gap between various individuals' stories. In our mind, what may be going on is "John is unreliable, and I cannot count on him to do his work" or "Alex is annoying and demanding and does not respect people's personal life." A more constructive way is to acknowledge that we have different views about this specific report. One person's view may be that this report is very important and needs to be done on time and as well as possible. The other person's view may be that this is just another work report and that it is important to establish boundaries around how much work is reasonable to expect in a short period. Once we are able to define the problem from a neutral point of view, we are better positioned to find a mutually acceptable solution. A neutral story acknowledges the disagreement in neutral terms – "We disagree regarding when we should work on this report" – and recognizes the differing perspectives – "We assign different priorities to this work." Through constructing a neutral story, we can look for solutions by negotiating deadlines, responsibilities, and possibly other commitments. For example, I may agree to work on this report tonight if I can have a day off on Friday. Or we may agree to complete a critical element of the report on time and postpone another component. These agreements are based on an acknowledgment of different needs and perspectives and focus on acceptable practices.

In summary, when facing a conflict, we need to start by assessing whether there is a difference of interpretations that can be solved through communication. Once misunderstandings are cleared, we can focus on understanding the nature of the conflict. Conflicts of tastes and preferences can be *avoided* through acceptance or compromise. When agreement is necessary it is better to focus on the practices, and attempt to construct the problem from a neutral point of view, sticking to the facts and differing interpretations without judgment or blame. Inquiry and advocacy may help construct a neutral story that will form the foundation for an agreement on how to move forward. Conflicts of values are the most challenging to deal with, and may be dealt with through a focus on practices and equifinal understandings.

The Road Ahead

We learn how to communicate through our experience in cultural communities. We learn how and when we are supposed to say what we think, and we learn protocols and formalities to facilitate communication and decrease what needs to be said. When we communicate with people from other cultures, the same behaviors and protocols that helped us ease communication within our culture may be a source of misunderstanding and frustration. We need to listen carefully, engage in inquiry and advocacy, and try different communication styles to establish a new common ground and reach a common understanding. Further, when misunderstanding is clear but conflict remains, we need to understand what the cause of the conflict is, in order to address it. However, success in dealing with ambiguous and messy intercultural interactions where people do not share understanding requires much more than communication tools; it also requires some serious internal work and a commitment to continuous intercultural development. Avenues for further development are discussed in the next chapter.

Reflective Exercise

This exercise invites you to reflect upon your communication style and skills. You have two options for this exercise. You can continue using the basic reflection guide focusing on communication, or you can use the variation of the double-column method to help you identify your own theories-of-action you may not be aware of and uncover problems with your communication.

Tell Your Story

Write a detailed description of an intercultural situation. Draw on all your senses and make your description as rich and detailed as possible. What was the context of this situation? Who was there? What was influencing your behavior? What did you say or do? What did others say or do? How were you feeling?

Consider details of your communication. What did you say? How did you say it? What did you not say? What did you assume to be known or understood?

Variation: The Double-Column Method

The double-column method is a learning tool directed at observing communication.[20] Start by thinking about a recent conversation in which you had to solve a problem through communication. The problem does not have to be important; it may be as simple as deciding on a meeting place. Write down your conversation in the table below (take extra paper if necessary). On the right-hand side write the dialogue – what you said and what the other person said. In the left-hand column write any idea, feeling, or assumption that you had but did not communicate, for whatever reason.

Thoughts	Dialogue

Revisit Your Story

Leave your story aside for at least one hour. Then, revisit your story by asking yourself the following questions:

✓ Are there facts, thoughts, or details not considered in your description that could change your interpretation of the story?
✓ What assumptions were guiding your actions? What knowledge might have influenced you?
✓ When interacting with others, what were you trying to achieve? Did you respond effectively? What were the consequences of your actions for others and yourself? What would be the consequences had you responded differently? What factors might prevent you from responding in new ways?
✓ How did you feel and why did you feel that way? How did your feelings influence your actions? What were others' feelings and why did they feel that way? How do you feel about this experience now?

✓ How does this situation connect with other experiences?

• What can you learn about how *you* communicate? How much of what you thought was communicated to the other party? Have you made assumptions they may not know about or share? Were you blaming the other party? Were you upsetting the other party? Could you have done anything differently?

• How different were the stories that you and your counterpart constructed? How would thinking about a neutral story change the way you communicate?

Prepare for the Future and Apply Learning

✓ What insights have you gained from this experience, and what are their implications for the future?

✓ Does this situation require further action? Of what kind? Are there things you need to say or do? Are there knowledge gaps you need to cover? How can you validate your conclusions?

✓ Based on what you have learned, how are you approaching new situations?

• Consider which questions you may need to ask now or in the future (inquiry).

• Consider what you need to explain, now or in the future (advocacy).

• Consider what sources of conflict may emerge.

Key Points

• Communication is at the core of intercultural interactions and the main mechanism for achieving intercultural understanding.

• Culture provides members with the *common ground* required to go about their everyday life. Common ground consists of mutually *known* – even if not uniformly agreed on – facts, beliefs, and assumptions about what is acceptable or not acceptable, desirable or undesirable.

• *Grounding* is the collective process by which individuals try to achieve the mutual belief that they have reached a level of

understanding that is *sufficient for current purposes.*
- Creating common ground relies on active listening, inquiry, and advocacy.
- *Inquiry* refers to a process of seeking new information to better understand the points of view of the people involved in an interaction. Inquiry refers to exploring and questioning our own reasoning and the reasoning of others to understand their interpretations.
- *Advocacy* refers to expressing and standing up for what one thinks and desires. Advocacy involves stating clearly what we think and want and explaining the reasoning behind our view.
- When dealing with conflicts, it is critical to understand the source of conflict. Conflicts of tastes and preferences can be avoided through acceptance or compromise. When agreement is necessary, it is better to focus on practices and attempt to construct the problem from a neutral point of view, sticking to the facts and differing interpretations without judgment or blame. Conflicts of values are the most challenging to deal with and may be dealt with through a focus on practices and equifinal understandings.

CHAPTER 9

Moving Forward

A young but earnest Zen student approached his teacher, and asked the Zen Master: "If I work very hard and diligently how long will it take for me to find Zen." The Master thought about this, and then replied, "Ten years." The student then said, "But what if I work very, very hard and really apply myself to learn fast – How long then?" Replied the Master, "Well, twenty years." "But, if I really, really work at it. How long then?" asked the student? "Thirty years," replied the Master. "But, I do not understand," said the disappointed student. "Each time that I say I will work harder, you say it will take me longer. Why do you say that?" Replied the Master, "When you have one eye on the goal, you only have one eye on the path."

Zen story[1]

The above Zen story is often used in the context of martial arts learning, implying that deep and transformative learning can't be rushed. At the end of a course or training program, or after reading a book like this, the most we can aspire to is to move forward on the path toward intercultural competence and identify the next step along the way. The infinite variety of intercultural interactions we may face and the high levels of ambiguity associated with them mean that, despite our best efforts, continuous reflection, and increased awareness, we will still encounter challenging situations, cultural misunderstandings, and frustrations and find ourselves sometimes doing the "wrong thing." These experiences do not need to be discouraging; instead they may help feed the cycle of increased learning and self-awareness. Developing intercultural competence is a *process*. It is not something that happens overnight. Intercultural competence requires a new way of thinking and approaching situations. Moreover, each situation is unique and presents new challenges. We eventually get good at some situations but will likely stumble with new situations at some point. Over time we may get better and deal with various intercultural experiences with ease, and may unexpectedly discover some of our blind spots. For example, we may think that we can deal with all types of people but find it difficult to deal with our neighbor who has strong prejudices or ideals we do not share. We may think we are very open-minded but can't accept the point of view of our colleagues. There are always some areas that we need to work on and develop. The purpose of this chapter is to suggest avenues for continuous development. First, however, it provides a brief review in order to integrate some of the main points discussed in this book.

Interacting in an Enacted World

Throughout, this book has explored the role of cultural background; of idiosyncratic individual characteristics, such as knowledge, skills, and preferences; and of context in influencing our behavior and intercultural interactions (see figure 9.1). It has also considered how behavior varies across contexts and how some situations make our cultural preferences salient while others suppress it. As we interact with others, our behaviors, including how and what we communicate and how and which emotions we express, shape our interactions in a dynamic process of action and reaction. Success in intercultural relations depends on a *process of interaction* to facilitate the development of common understanding and agreement on

Figure 9.1 Intercultural interactions

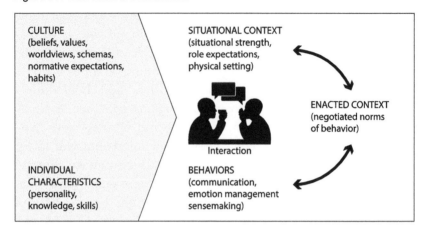

norms of behavior and to create a positive context. A review of some helpful steps toward this end follows.

1. Developing Self- and Situational Awareness

Thinking of an intercultural interaction as a process of continuous sensemaking and co-creation of our situations suggests that we must be *constantly* aware of ourselves, the other, and the evolving interaction. That is, we must constantly pay attention to what we are feeling and doing, what the other is feeling and doing, and how the other reacts to what we say and do. In the process of learning about the other and testing ways to interact, *we need to be aware of our own behavior and the effects of our behavior on others.* When we are aware of our cultural resources, strengths, and weaknesses and are sensitive to the demands and constraints of our situation, we can reposition ourselves to take advantage of our resources.

Toward this end, a critical skill is the ability to *take perspective* – to see things from a point of view different from our own. We need to attempt to understand how others with whom we are interacting see a situation – getting "inside their heads" to comprehend why they concluded what they did. When we are able to see the situation from the other person's point of view, we may gain significant insights into our own and others' behavior. When facing a puzzling thought or behavior, some helpful questions might be: "What would a reasonable person have to assume or believe to come to this conclusion?" "What would I have to believe to agree with them?" You might also ask: "What do I assume or believe that makes my conclusion reasonable?"

2. Managing Identities and Emotions

Intercultural interactions challenge our long-established belief systems, perspectives, and assumptions about right and wrong. This process is likely to elicit strong feelings. We need to grapple with challenges to *our own competence, worth, and character* (and so do our counterparts). Thus, managing the process of an intercultural interaction needs to involve a resolution of the participants' identities and feelings. My experience with business students and professionals is that they often prefer to focus on "business," avoiding the emotional components of an interaction and favoring an over-rational analysis of the situation. However, this focus on the "objective" and the "rational" is misplaced, given that people's interpretations of issues and solutions *are* influenced by their emotions and self-image. Management scholar Gerard Hodgkinson and colleagues suggest that the transformation of mindsets and behaviors required not only for intercultural competence but also for innovative activities and other change processes can't be understood through a focus on "cold-cognition." Rather, emotional management is a critical and often overlooked aspect of organizational life.[2]

Thus, we must acknowledge that our differing views can't always be solved by rational arguments alone, and that we need to be sensitive to the feelings that arise for all parties involved. We need to *empathetically* work with the other to construct a neutral story that includes how we feel about the issues at hand and preserves how we feel about ourselves.

3. Negotiating Understanding by Constructing a Neutral Story

The main goal of an intercultural interaction is to develop enough understanding to facilitate agreement on how to move forward. In other words, we need to co-construct a story of our situation from a neutral point of view, sticking to the facts and differing interpretations without judgment or blame. *Inquiry* (exploring and questioning one's own reasoning and the reasoning of others) and *advocacy* (expressing what we think and want and explaining our reasoning) can help construct this neutral story as we clarify assumptions, perceptions, and expectations.

Engaging in inquiry and advocacy is challenging because it requires uncovering our own perceptions, exposing ourselves, being open to listening to others' perceptions, and being willing to give up the safety of our own previous interpretations in order for a new, culture-neutral interpretation to emerge. Further, the process of inquiry and advocacy must be adjusted depending on the cultural and situational context of an interaction. We must gather information in several different ways, relying on context, body language, subtle cues, and messages, as well as direct questioning.

4. Managing Context

When we understand that awareness of norms and expectations will emerge through interaction, we may recognize ways in which we can take purposeful action toward facilitating understanding. We may look for opportunities to leverage and manage differences through deliberate efforts to construct a positive context for the interaction. Some cultural and individual differences, such as differences in knowledge, skills, and interpretations, are a source of opportunity that can be leveraged. Others, such as normative expectations, values, and preferences may be a source of conflict.

In ambiguous situations, we are more likely to rely on our own assumptions about what is appropriate behavior. Ambiguity may be decreased by clearly articulating norms of behavior within the context, using artifacts or cues. On the other hand, differences in perspective that are critical for advancing our goals (such as different market or cultural knowledge) must be purposefully brought to the forefront to be leveraged and benefit the team or organization.

Continuous Development

When discussing how one becomes a good writer, science fiction author Ray Bradbury said, "An athlete must run a thousand miles to prepare for one hundred yards."[3] Developing any skill worth having takes practice, and intercultural competence is one of those skills. Engaging in intercultural experiences of various types is critical both to gain exposure to different people, ideas, and perspectives and to gain insight into our own culture, our own skills, and ourselves. Learning how to make sense of secondhand information is also important.

Engaging in Intercultural Experiences

Many people think of worthwhile intercultural experiences as those involving extensive travel in exotic locations. While those experiences are worth having, they are not necessarily more useful for the development of intercultural competence than other less exotic encounters with other cultures. As interculturalist Joseph Shaules has noted, "It's not the distance travelled that matters; it is the *depth* of our experience that counts."[4] There are a couple of reasons for this. First, when we travel to faraway places, we often adopt the attitude of a tourist. While we may be curious about other ways of life, we tend to hop around between many different sites and to consume a significant amount of culture that is prepared for tourists' consumption but may have little resemblance to the life of the local people. As we move between tourist spots, often with a group of people of our own culture, we may have little – if any – engagement with local people outside of a touristic exchange. As a friend said about his recent trip to Paris, "I don't know if I will ever have the opportunity to go to Paris again so I wanted to see as many sites as I could in the four days I was visiting." In these cases, we interact primarily with tourism workers such as guides and hotel personnel, and engage in commercial activities dedicated to tourism; but we seldom interact with local people living a local life.

Second, by hopping from one tourist destination to another we get overwhelmed with sounds, colors, and sights and may not consider the effects this experience has on our thinking and behavior. A good intercultural experience should allow for the uncovering of hidden assumptions and the restructuring of patterns of thinking. When traveling abroad and consuming culture in the form of music and dance performances and local cuisine, and observing the way people dress and behave in specific sites, look around and observe who else is there. Do you see local people in the audience? What are local people doing? Seek local activities and observe how the local people interact, what they do, and how they relate to one another. There are many tourist attractions that supposedly show the ways of life of a community. It is important to keep in mind that these communities receive tourists on a regular basis and understand the importance of "performing" a culture that is attractive to tourists' eyes. That culture, while real, is not the culture one needs to understand to develop intercultural skills.

When traveling abroad in order to develop intercultural skills, it is important to stray from the beaten path and experience the foreign location through the eyes of the local people. That may mean getting into a crowded and unpleasant bus, skipping the fancy restaurants and eating where the local people eat, engaging with the local people, and attempting to understand their way of life. To develop intercultural skills, we need to interact with people with different points of view for a common purpose. It is a shift from *watching* to *engaging*. A worthwhile experience exposes us to different ideas, uncovers our hidden assumptions and beliefs, and is a catalyst for transformation.

Consider your last tourist trip. How did you approach your travel planning? What were you focused on doing/seeing/learning? How did you do that? How much did you engage with the local culture? To what extent did you have an opportunity to appreciate the local way of life?

Transformational experiences may also happen close to home. It is possible to have meaningful and developmental intercultural experiences without traveling, by seeking out people from other cultures who have immigrated or are visiting, or by engaging with foreign cultural ideas. At home, our opportunities to experience other cultures may be limited, but it is possible to develop intercultural competence by considering *one cultural idea at a time* and exploring how that idea is related to the way we do things. For example, by spending time with a local immigrant community, we may learn about their views on family, work, or any other issue of interest. As we consider these ideas and perspectives we have the opportunity to slowly consider our own views and assumptions. Seeking people and circumstances that will expose us to our own cultural assumptions is a good way to expand our cultural boundaries and start the development process. This may mean engaging in cross-religious dialogue, seeking to understand cultural traditions that seem foreign to us, or learning arts and practices from other cultures. The key is to think about *intercultural interactions as learning opportunities*.

When we think of intercultural interactions as learning opportunities, we focus on understanding rather than judging. Instead of approaching an idea asking, "Do I like it or not?," we approach cultural elements with curiosity and respect. While some things may seem crazy or illogical, they *are* logical from the point of view of members of a cultural group. Success in intercultural situations requires an appreciation of the fact that even though we may not *like* a point of view (and it is okay not to like it) this point of view still *makes sense* within the context of the culture where it was created.

We have all been guilty of ethnocentrism at some point – that is, of judging another culture by the standards of our own culture.[5] This is normal, as we use what we know to make sense of our new experiences. Culture provides us with the mental infrastructure to make sense of things, giving us categories that help us make connections and understand the characteristics, functions, and uses of objects and beings. Through culture we learn if a guinea pig is a pet, a pest, or lunch. When we are faced with a different culture in which things are categorized differently, we may have a deep, gut-level reaction to the discrepancies we face (how can someone eat a guinea pig?). These instances in which we face discrepancies are learning opportunities on the road toward intercultural competence. It is in these instances that we can choose to shut down and judge the other or take a deep breath and open ourselves up to the possibility of new understanding.

In summary, practice, in the form of mindful engagement with people and ideas from other cultures, is a key component of the development of intercultural competence. However, practice, to be effective, requires not only experiencing but also reflecting on our experiences and allowing ourselves to learn and change (see a comprehensive reflection guide in appendix B). Developing intercultural competence requires us to reconsider deep-seated beliefs and assumptions, a process that takes considerable time and effort. Our goal is, first, to become aware of our beliefs and assumptions, to accept them, and then gently and nonjudgmentally explore how they influence our ability to interact effectively with others.

Cultural Information[6]

As we engage in intercultural experiences and reflect on them, we often find gaps in our knowledge and need to seek additional cultural information. For instance, imagine a great professional opportunity that requires you to travel to Namibia, Kyrgyzstan, or Suriname. Depending on where you live and your personal life experiences, you may not be familiar with any of these countries and their cultures, in which case you may quickly search online to find out more about them. If, after some initial searches, you are still intrigued, you might go to your social media accounts and check if anyone in your network has any connections in these countries.

Internet technology is changing our relationship to each other and to information. These changes are sometimes depicted as good (the world is at our fingertips; how else could you find out that there are more than twenty million Muslims living in China?) and sometimes as bad (we are replacing real friendships with Facebook friends). Regardless of how we feel about these changes, the reality is that our intercultural understanding is heavily influenced by what is happening online.

Nowadays, there is a proliferation of easily accessible cultural information from diverse sources. Technology allows any individual with Internet access to generate and consume intercultural information easily, and this information remains visible and accessible to others over time. For example, travel or expatriate bloggers write about their cultural experiences at their convenience, for their own purposes, and without the constraints experienced by more official sources, such as the staff and publications of immigration offices, educators, and not-for-profit organizations (e.g., as to style, topic, claims, sources, accuracy, or truthfulness).

As a result, when searching for information, we may access outdated information (such as posts written in the past about events or situations that are no longer relevant), decontextualized information (such as information that applies to a very specific context but is presented as generalizable), biased information (such as points of view that are based on a one-sided perspective), conflicting information (contradictory versions of the same event), and plain wrong or false information. Consequently, the abundant information environment afforded by technology is fraught with contradictions, misinformation, biases, and generalizations that may hinder our ability to work across cultures. When consuming cultural information, we need to be critical and evaluate the degree to which the information is relevant to our current contexts and the degree to which the information source is reliable.

Intercultural competence in the digital age requires the ability to probe for details and assess the validity of cultural information, seeking disconfirming evidence before accepting cultural depictions as given. In other words, we must be able to separate *facts* from *interpretations* and assess whether those facts and interpretations are relevant for our needs. For example, in our research on expatriate bloggers, my co-authors and I found that bloggers conveyed their understanding of Canadian norms of politeness, speech, and standing in line; their values surrounding friendship, body image, multiculturalism, and ways of life; and their views on the Canadian institutions that govern education, health, and work practices. The bloggers' experiences, interpretations, and conclusions were highly personal and not always representative of Canadian culture.[7] To benefit from reading this body of information we need to be critical and able to distinguish what is fact (e.g., immigration laws, demographic composition of a community) from what is opinion (e.g., Canadians are – or are not – friendly).

An additional risk associated with overreliance on easily available sources of information is the risk of confusing saliency with importance. Some issues receive disproportionate attention and are highly salient. As a result, they may seem more important than they really are, while other less salient issues may be ignored. As each situation is unique, there is no guarantee that the salient issues are the ones that are most relevant to our situation. As we search for cultural information online, notice who is writing and consider whether biases or misrepresentations may be present. Notice which issues are salient, and consider which issues may not be receiving enough attention.

Easily accessible online information may be a good source of knowledge about other cultures, provided we are able to critically evaluate its relevance to our own experiences. It is worth pointing out that Internet technology also offers the possibility to engage with other cultures virtually. In addition to consuming what other people have posted, we can engage with other cultural communities and experience other cultures virtually by participating in community discussions, communicating with others, or visiting places virtually.

These experiences may provide a platform for the further development of intercultural competence, provided we are mindful of how the virtual context may be influencing the experience.

Concluding Thoughts

Possessing intercultural competence does not mean that we do not judge, react, or feel negative emotions when interacting with other cultures. Rather, it means we have the ability to *notice* when thoughts and feelings we are experiencing are not helping us behave in ways that facilitate cooperation and understanding, and to *engage* with our thoughts and feelings in order to identify better courses of action, including withdrawing from a situation until we are better able to deal with it.

Intercultural competence is not a trait; it is a skill. Some days we are better able to apply our skills than others, and our skills will evolve and change over time. Some days or situations may find us tired, frustrated, and less able to notice the nuances of what is going on or to deal with them skillfully. We may know what we need to do but may be tired or impatient and unable to be our best self. As we practice working across cultural boundaries, we gain awareness of our own ability to deal with difficult situations, come to understand our own limitations, and become better able to deal with them. It may be, for example, that you realize that if you adapt to the norm of consuming copious amounts of alcohol in business meetings that is common in some Asian countries, you will be less able to deal with other cultural issues that arise during the meeting. You can then to decide which course of action makes more sense to you in a given situation.

The Road Ahead

In the multicultural reality of today's workplace, we are likely to face many ambiguous and sometimes difficult situations. This book has examined many qualities and/or competencies we can develop to improve our ability to deal with such situations – cultural self-awareness, situational awareness, communication skills, sensemaking skills, and the ability to manage feelings – and has identified some avenues for further learning. These qualities/competencies are not only useful for dealing with people who hold different passports from our own. Rather, they are skills that can help us navigate a world full of boundaries and differences.

Consider the messy world problems we are facing today: climate change, environmental issues, starvation and obesity, wars and conflicts, and the list goes on – issues that are overwhelmingly complex and difficult to solve and that affect billions of people. But they all have one thing in common: the solution to these problems requires a coordinated effort of people with very different perspectives. None of these problems can be solved by one group of people alone, looking at the issue from just one perspective. If there was one perspective everyone agreed on, we would not have the problems in the first place. What has hampered us is our general inability to cross over to the other side, to give up the certainty of our individual perspectives, and to accept that there may be another way to understand the world – one that is different from our own.

This is where intercultural competence comes in. As we learn to work with each other, and learn from each other, we may start to appreciate our differences not as a source of problems and conflict but as a source of enrichment and synergy. When we open up to learn from each other and let go of our preconceived ideas of how the world should work, we can create a better place for all of us.

Reflective Exercise

In this last reflective exercise, you are invited to consider your journey so far and think of ways to make reflection an integral part of your life. You do not need to write a new story. Rather, go back and reread your reflections with an open and curious mind.

Revisit your Reflections

Revisit your reflections by asking yourself how what you have written can help or has helped you increase your intercultural competence. Consider the assumptions that were guiding your thoughts and actions and how they have changed (or not). Consider your feelings then and now. Consider what you knew then and what you know now.

Prepare for the Future and Apply Learning

- Consider the insights you have gained and their implications for the future. Based on what you have learned, how are you approaching new situations?
- How can you continue your path toward intercultural development? How can you engage more in intercultural experiences? How can you make better use of cultural information?

Key Points

- Intercultural interactions are facilitated when we are able to develop self- and situational awareness, manage identities and emotions, construct a neutral story, and manage context to decrease ambiguity and misunderstanding.
- Engaging in intercultural experiences of various types is critical to developing intercultural competence, as such experiences expose us to different people, ideas, and perspectives and give us insight into ourselves, our cultures, and our skills. What matters in an intercultural experience is the depth of the experience, not how different the cultures are.
- Cultural information is important but needs to be carefully evaluated for relevance and accuracy, and in order to separate facts from interpretations.

Cross-cultural Studies

While comparing cultural dimensions provides only a thumbnail sketch of some general trends in variations between two or more societal cultures, it can be useful as a starting point for reflecting upon our own culture. The goal here is not to provide an extensive review of models of national culture, or a definitive set of characteristics for classifying people. Rather, I invite you to be curious and consider how you feel about each of these dimensions. I am presenting themes that have emerged from well-researched dimensions of culture as a way to facilitate cultural self-awareness and provide you with some structure in the exploration of the role of culture in your life. The original studies that identified these dimensions are summarized at the end of this section. As you reflect on how you feel about each of the cultural themes described below, keep in mind that our feelings may differ from one situation to another. The important thing is to reflect on how and when some of our values or beliefs become important.

Theme 1: Power Distribution

Beliefs and expectations regarding how power should be distributed in society and organizations emerge in several studies of culture.

Typically, these norms are expressed in terms of whether power should be centralized at or near the top of a hierarchy (usually referred to as *hierarchical* or *high power distance* cultures) or distributed in a more egalitarian fashion (usually referred to as *egalitarian* or *low power distance* cultures). While the notion of power distribution was initially conceived as a societal level dimension, we can observe significant variations in the distribution of power within organizations in the same society. For example, military organizations tend to be more hierarchical than universities. Consider your own society and organization: How is power distributed? How much power do managers have *vis-à-vis* subordinates? How much power do women have *vis-à-vis* men? How easy is it to move between ranks? Why?

Anthropologist Edward Hall also identified power as an important cultural issue but conceptualized it slightly differently. The dimension he identified refers to the way people are comfortable sharing physical space. One extreme sees the center of power as *territorial*, where people have needs for clearly delineated personal spaces. On the other end, the center of power is *communal* and people are comfortable sharing their personal space. When speaking with others, how far from the other person do you feel most comfortable? (At arm's length? Farther away? Closer?) How do you feel when someone moves closer? How do you feel when someone uses your desk or sits on your favorite chair? Why?

Theme 2: Time

The way people approach time has also emerged as an important difference across cultures. Some researchers have focused on how the past and the future (or short and long term views) influence our decisions. People in cultures oriented toward the *past* are influenced by tradition and past events and have a high regard for their ancestors and traditions. People in *future*-oriented cultures are more concerned with planning for future possibilities and tend to value hard work, persistence, thrift, and dedication.

Anthropologist Edward Hall took a different approach to time, and one that resonates with anyone trying to get things done across borders. Hall observed that in some cultures, called *monochronic* cultures, people tend to be methodical in their use of time and their approach to tasks. They see time as a commodity that can be measured, used, and sometimes sold. In monochronic cultures, people are often concerned about *wasting time*. They often approach work as a series of tasks or goals that should be tackled sequentially, one at a time. By contrast, people in more *polychronic* cultures tend to be more flexible, addressing several problems simultaneously. They are less concerned with time and resist firm deadlines. They also tend to mix work and personal lives in a more fluid fashion than their monochronic counterparts, who stress a clear separation between work and non-work situations.

Consider: how do you feel when people are late for an appointment? How often are you late for appointments? How late is too late? If you have a meeting at 9:00 a.m., when do you consider that someone is late? Does it change by context? Imagine that you are going to a meeting and a colleague you have not seen lately stops you in the hallway and starts what could potentially become a long conversation. Do you engage in the conversation and arrive late to your meeting or tell your colleague you are running late and will catch up later? Why?

Theme 3: Social Relationships

The influence of culture on the way we deal with each other is clearly the most studied aspect of cultural differences. Many different cultural models identify a variation around the degree to which individuals or collectives take precedence. This dimension of culture affects the nature of social relationships and perceptions of self-identity. This dimension is usually expressed in terms of cultures being more *individualistic* or *collectivistic*. The distinction here is whether members of a society see themselves primarily as individuals or as members of a group. *Individualistic* cultures are based on the belief that social structures should be arranged based on individuals. Individual needs and interests should have precedence over group interests; individuals strive to be independent and autonomous and are responsible for themselves. *Collectivistic* cultures, on the other hand, are based on the belief that the basic unit of social structure is the group. Group interests take precedence over individual interests, group welfare is more important than individual independence, and individuals are seen as *interdependent*.

Edward Hall identified a dimension that, while apparently different, is related to the notion of individualism and collectivism. He identified that cultures vary in the way they communicate. In *low context* cultures people tend to be direct and frank, and the words of the message convey most of the meaning. In *high context* cultures, on the other hand, people rely on the context surrounding a message to communicate meaning. That is, the message is subtle, and what is said is not nearly as important as *how* it is said. A person may be saying "yes" but meaning "no," or vice versa, and relying on the context of the communication for the true meaning to be understood. In high context cultures, people rely on a high level of common ground and shared understanding. People express their individual opinions very subtly so as to not upset the social order. In individualistic cultures, which emphasize autonomy and independence, people favor open and frank communication. People are expected to "speak their minds," and there is less expectation of conformity.

Think about how you communicate: do you say what is in your mind or do you rely on other people's ability to read between the lines to really understand what you mean? Why?

Theme 4: Social Control

A final theme emerging in studies of culture involves the relative importance of rules versus relationships as a means of reducing uncertainty in society. In *rule-oriented* cultures there is little tolerance for ambiguity, and rules are used to constrain uncertainty and create a sense of predictability. Social interactions tend to be formalized, agreements documented, and records meticulously kept, and there is an abundance of rules and formal policies. As a result, in these cultures there is a tendency to promulgate a multitude of laws, rules, regulations, bureaucratic procedures, and strict social norms in an attempt to control as many unanticipated events or behaviors as possible. People tend to conform to officially sanctioned constraints because of a moral belief in the virtue of the rule of law and will often obey directives even if they know violations will not be detected. An example would be a pedestrian waiting for a red light in the absence of any traffic. Rules and laws are universally applied (at least in theory), with few exceptions for extenuating circumstances or personal connections. Things are done "by the book," and infractions often bring immediate sanctions or consequences. Finally, decisions tend to be made based on objective criteria to the extent possible. All of this is aimed at creating a society with no surprises.

Relationship-oriented cultures have a higher tolerance for ambiguity than rule-oriented cultures and do not feel the need for as many rules. Social interactions tend to be more informal; people rely on trust as opposed to contracts and have less concern for record keeping. These cultures tend to use influential people more than abstract or objective rules and regulations as a means of social control. This personal control can come from parents, peers, superiors, supervisors, government officials, and so forth – from anyone with influence over the individual. There is generally less record keeping and things tend to be done on an informal basis. There is also greater tolerance for noncompliance with bureaucratic rules in the belief that formal rules cannot cover all contingencies and that some flexibility is often required. Finally, decisions tend to be made based on a combination of objective and subjective criteria and with less formality.

Organizational scholar and consultant Fons Trompenaars has identified a related dimension dealing with the extent to which people see the importance of applying standardized rules and policies across societal members. In *universalistic* cultures, people rely on formal rules and policies that are applied equally to everyone. In *particularistic* cultures, rules must be tempered by the nature of the situation and the people involved. A typical example used to describe this dilemma is the confrontation between a driver and a pedestrian.[1] Imagine that you are riding in a car driven by a close friend and he hits a pedestrian. You know he was driving too fast in a limited speed zone. You are also aware that there are no other witnesses, and your friend's lawyer asks you to testify that he was actually driving within the speed limit. Indeed, if you testify honestly to his actual speed at the time of the accident, your friend will face serious legal consequences. What would you do? A purely universalistic view would suggest that you testify against your friend because "the law is the law." A more particularist view would temper the importance of the law based on the strength of the relationship with your friend.

Consider: to what extent is your behavior guided by rules and regulations? How much importance do you attach to contracts, record keeping, and written rules as opposed to trust and relationships? Why? How is people's behavior controlled in your work environment – through supervision or clear rules?

Theme 5: People and the Environment

Culture scholars have observed that societies have different views with respect to their relationship to their surroundings. These views deal with beliefs about the need or responsibility to control nature as well as the degree to which achievement and competitiveness are rewarded. While there is disagreement regarding the degree to which control and achievement are combined or independent, they suggest two important issues that are worth reflecting upon.

The first issue refers to our beliefs about our responsibility toward nature. In some cultures, usually referred to as *mastery* cultures, people believe that they should control nature, changing their environment to advance personal or group interests. In others, usually referred to as *harmony* cultures, people believe that they should work with nature to maintain balance, accepting and adapting to the world around them and attempting to preserve it. Consider: do you believe you should control or adapt to nature?

The second related issue deals with appropriate goals for human activities. Scholars have used different nomenclatures (see table A.1 at the end of this section) to deal with the degree to which cultures emphasize achievement. At one extreme, people value assertiveness, achievement, competitiveness, and domination. At the other extreme, people are more concerned with quality of life, belonging, and the welfare of others. A key issue here is whether there is an emphasis on material possessions as a symbol of achievement as opposed to a focus on economy, harmony, and societal sustainability. Consider: how important is achievement to you? How do you feel about assertiveness? Why? Does your response change by context?

Table A.1. Foundational cultural studies

	Kluckhohn and Strodtbeck[2]	Hofstede[3]	Schwartz[4]
Summary	One of the earliest models of culture and foundation for several later models. Argued that there are a limited number of problems that are common to all human groups and for which there are a limited number of solutions. Identified five value orientations, four of which were tested in five subcultures of the American Southwest.	Widely used model of cultural differences. Model was derived from a study of employees from various countries working for a major multinational corporation and based on the assumption that different cultures can be distinguished based on differences in what they value.	Model suggested that the essential distinction between societal values is the motivational goals they express. Identified ten universal human values that reflect needs, social motives, and social institutional demands purportedly found in all cultures and representing universal needs of human existence.
Power distribution		*Power distance*: Extent to which people accept and expect power to be distributed unequally (high) or attempt to equalize power distribution (low)	*Hierarchy-egalitarianism*: Extent to which equality is valued and expected
Time	*Relationship with time*: Extent to which past, present, and future influence decisions	*Long-term versus short-term orientation*: Extent to which people focus on past and present (short term) or future (long term)	

Hall[5]	Trompenaars[6]	GLOBE[7]
Model of culture based on his ethnographic research in several societies, notably Germany, France, the United States, and Japan. Focused primarily on how cultures vary in interpersonal communication, but also included work on personal space and time.	Model of culture based on a study of managers over a ten-year period. Model was based on the early work of sociologist Talcott Parsons and focused on variations in both values and personal relationships across cultures.	One of the most ambitious efforts to study cultural dimensions, in which an international team of researchers focused primarily on understanding the influence of cultural differences on leadership processes. Their investigation was called the "GLOBE study" (for Global Leadership and Organizational Behavior Effectiveness).
Space: Extent to which people are comfortable sharing physical space with others	*Achievement-ascription*: Degree to which respect and social status are accorded to people through achievement or ascription	*Power distance*: Degree to which people expect power to be distributed equally *Gender egalitarianism*: Degree to which gender differences are minimized
Time: Extent to which people approach one task at a time or multiple tasks simultaneously	*Time perspective*: Extent to which people focus on past and present or future	*Future orientation*: Extent to which people engage in future-oriented behaviors such as planning, investing, and delayed gratification

Table A.1. Foundational cultural studies (*continued*)

	Kluckhohn and Strodtbeck[2]	Hofstede[3]	Schwartz[4]
Social Relationships	*Relationship with people*: Beliefs about social structure	*Individualism-collectivism*: Relative importance of individual versus group interests	*Conservatism-autonomy*: Extent to which individuals are integrated in groups
Social control	*Human nature*: Beliefs about good, neutral, or evil human nature	*Uncertainty avoidance*: Degree of uncertainty that can be tolerated and its impact on rule making	
People and environment	*Relationship with nature*: Beliefs about the need or responsibility to control nature *Human activities:* Beliefs about appropriate goals: being, becoming, and doing	*Masculinity-femininity*: Assertiveness versus passivity; material possessions versus quality of life	*Mastery-harmony*: Extent to which people seek to change the natural and social world to advance personal or group interests
Others		*Indulgence versus restraint*: degree to which a culture allows free gratification of basic and natural human drives[8]	

Hall[5]	Trompenaars[6]	GLOBE[7]
Context: Extent to which the context of a message is as important as the message itself	*Individualism-collectivism*: Extent to which people derive their identity from within themselves or from their group	*Institutional collectivism*: Extent to which society encourages collective distribution of resources and collective action *In-group collectivism*: Extent to which individuals express pride, loyalty, and cohesiveness in their organizations and families
	Universalism-particularism: Relative importance of applying standardized rules and policies across societal members; role of exceptions in rule enforcement	*Uncertainty avoidance*: Extent to which people rely on norms, rules, and procedures to reduce the unpredictability of future events
	Relationship with environment: Extent to which people believe they control their environment or it controls them	*Assertiveness*: Degree to which people are assertive, confrontational, and aggressive in relationships with others *Performance orientation*: Degree to which high performance is encouraged and rewarded *Humane orientation*: Extent to which people reward fairness, altruism, and generosity
	Specific-diffuse: Extent to which people's various roles are compartmentalized or integrated *Neutral-affective*: Extent to which people are free to express their emotions in public	.

Comprehensive Reflection Assignment

Below you will find a comprehensive reflection exercise incorporating all topics covered in the book.

Tell Your Story
Write a detailed description of an intercultural situation you have experienced. Draw on all your senses and make your description as rich and detailed as possible. What was the context of this situation? Who was there? What was influencing your behavior? What did you say or do? What did others say or do? How were you feeling?

Revisit Your Story
Revisit your story by asking yourself the following questions:

• Are there facts, thoughts, or details not considered in your description that could change your interpretation of the story?
• What assumptions were guiding your actions? What knowledge might have influenced you? What values or norms guided your behavior and your interpretation of the situation? Was your behavior normal for you? Was your behavior typical of others of your cultural background? Why or why not?

- When interacting with others, what were you trying to achieve? Did you respond effectively? What were the consequences of your actions for others and yourself? What would have been the consequences if you had responded differently? What factors might prevent you from responding in new ways?
- In what ways did the context enable or hinder this interaction? Did you respond effectively given the characteristics of the context? Could you have had a positive influence in this context? Did you? What could you have done to make other people's experience of this context better? What was your role in shaping the dynamics of the interaction? In what ways have you influenced the behavior of others? How did you change the nature of the interaction?
- How much of what you thought was communicated to the other party? Did you make assumptions they might not know about or share? Were you blaming the other party? Were you upsetting the other party? Could you have done anything differently? How different were the stories that you and your counterpart constructed? How would thinking about a neutral story change the way you communicated?
- How did you feel and why did you feel that way? How did your feelings influence your actions? What were others' feelings and why did they feel that way? How do you feel about this experience now? To what extent have your feelings constrained your ability to respond effectively? To what extent have you demonstrated empathy toward the other? How can this situation be reframed positively? How would a more positive outlook allow you to respond differently?
- How does this situation connect with other experiences?

Prepare for the Future
- What insights have you gained from this experience and what are their implications for the future?
- Does this situation require further action? Of what kind? Are there things you need to say or do? Are there knowledge gaps you need to cover? How can you validate your conclusions?

- Based on what you have learned, how are you approaching new situations?

Notes

Preface

1 Julia Cameron, *The Artist's Way: A Spiritual Path to Higher Creativity* (New York: Jeremy P. Tarcher/Putnam, 2002).
2 K.E. Weick, K.M. Sutcliffe, and D. Obstfeld, "Organizing and the Process of Sensemaking," *Organization Science* 16.4 (2005): 416.

Chapter 1. Working in a Multicultural World

1 Migration Policy Institute, *International Migration Statistics: International Migrants by Country of Destination, 1960–2013.* Retrieved 2 February 2015 from:http://www.migrationpolicy.org/programs/data-hub/international-migration-statistics.
2 Finnacord, *Global Expatriates: Size, Segmentation and Forecast for the Worldwide Market.* Retrieved 2 February 2015 from: http://www.finaccord.com/press-release_2014_global-expatriates_-size-segmentation-and-forecast-for-the-worldwide-market.htm.
3 Joseph J. Distefano and Martha L. Maznevski, "Creating Value with Diverse Teams in Global Management," *Organizational Dynamics* 29.10 (2000): 45–63.
4 Anne N. Pieterse, Daan V. Knippenberg, and Dirk Van Dierendonck, "Cultural Diversity and Team Performance: The Role of Team Member Goal Orientation," *Academy of Management Journal* 56.3 (2013): 782–804.
5 Richard Steers, Carlos Sanchez-Runde, and Luciara Nardon, *Managing across Cultures: Challenges and Strategies* (Cambridge: Cambridge University Press, 2010), 241.
6 Victor J. Friedman, and Ariane Berthoin Antal, "Negotiating Reality: A Theory of Action Approach to Intercultural Competence," *Management Learning* 36 (2005): 69.

7 Stefanie Rathje, "Intercultural Competence: The Status and Future of a
   Controversial Concept," *Language and Intercultural Communication* 7.4
   (2007): 254–66; David C. Thomas, "Domain and Development of Cultural
   Intelligence: The Importance of Mindfulness," *Group & Organization
   Management* 31.1 (2006): 78–99.
8 Edward W. Taylor, "A Learning Model for Becoming Interculturally
   Competent," *International Journal of Intercultural Relations* 18.3 (1994):
   389–408; Jack Mezirow, "How Critical Reflection Triggers Transformative
   Learning," in Jack Mezirow, ed., *Fostering Critical Reflection in Adulthood:
   A Guide to Transformative and Emancipatory Learning*, 1–20 (San Francisco:
   Jossey-Bass, 1990).
9 Linda Hill, *Building Effective One-on-One Work Relationships* (Watertown,
   MA: Harvard Business Publishing, 1996).
10 Philip N. Johnson-Laird, *Mental Models: Towards a Cognitive Science of
   Language, Inference, and Consciousness* (Cambridge, MA: Harvard
   University Press, 1983).
11 Valerie Rosenblatt, Reginald Worthley, and Brent MacNab, "From Contact to
   Development in Experiential Cultural Intelligence Education: The Mediating
   Influence of Expectancy Disconfirmation," *Academy of Management: Learning
   & Education* 12.3 (2013): 356–79.
12 Paula Caligiuri, "Developing Culturally Agile Global Business Leaders,"
   Organizational Dynamics 42 (2013): 175–82.
13 Craig C. Lundberg, "Is There Really Nothing So Practical as a Good
   Theory?" *Business Horizons* 47.5 (2004): 7–14.
14 Readers interested in an introductory overview of cultural differences and
   their workplace implications may refer to Steers, Sanchez-Runde, and
   Nardon, *Managing across Cultures.*
15 A. Haglage, "Kissing the Corpses in Ebola Country," *Daily Beast,* 13 August
   2014; retrieved 4 March 2015 from: http://www.thedailybeast.com/
   articles/2014/08/13/kissing-the-corpses-in-ebola-country.html.
16 Chimamanda N. Adichie, "The Danger of a Single Story." Posted October
   2009, *TED Talks;* retrieved 21 June 2016 from: https://www.ted.com/
   talks/chimamanda_adichie_the_danger_of_a_single_story/transcript?
   language=en.
17 Friedman and Berthoin Antal, "Negotiating Reality."

Chapter 2. Building Intercultural Competence through Reflection

1 Giada Di Stefano, Francesca Gino, Gary Pisano, and Bradley Staats,
   "Learning by Thinking: How Reflection Aids Performance," *HBS Working
   Paper Series* (2014): 14–93.

2 D.K. Deardorff, "Identification and Assessment of Intercultural Competence as a Student Outcome of Internationalization," *Journal of Studies in International Education* 10. 3 (2006): 241–66; Darla K. Deardorff, "Assessing Intercultural Competence," *New Directions for Institutional Research* 149 (2011): 65–79; Kok-Yee Ng, Linn Van Dyne, and Soon Ang, "From Experience to Experiential Learning: Cultural Intelligence as a Learning Capability for Global Leader Development," *Academy of Management Learning & Education* 8.4 (2009): 511–26.

3 Gillie Bolton, *Reflective Practice: Writing & Professional Development* (Thousand Oaks, CA: Sage Publications, 2010).

4 Richard Winter, "Fictional-Critical Writing," in J. Nias and S. Grondwater-Smith, eds., *The Enquiring Teacher* (London: Falmer, 1988), 235.

5 David E. Gray, "Facilitating Management Learning – Developing Critical Reflection through Reflective Tools," *Management Learning* 38.5 (2007): 495–517.

6 Karl E. Weick, *Sensemaking in Organizations* (Thousand Oaks, CA: Sage Publications, 1995).

7 Ibid., 128.

8 This quotation as well as other blog quotations cited in this chapter were identified through a large study I conducted with my colleague Kathryn Aten. We analyzed 606 blog posts written by expatriates and immigrants living in Canada to understand their adjustment experience. This quotation is from a study of bloggers' reflections published in Luciara Nardon and Kathryn Aten, "Making Sense of a Foreign Culture through Technology: Triggers, Mechanisms, and Introspective Focus in Newcomers' Blogs," *International Journal of Intercultural Relations* 54 (2016): 18. Subsequent quotations from the initial study will be identified simply as extracts from the study by Nardon and Aten; specific page numbers will not necessarily be given each time.

9 Christopher Johns, *Becoming a Reflective Practitioner* (Hoboken, NJ: John Wiley & Sons, 2013).

10 Anthony Weston, *A Rulebook for Arguments*, 4th ed. (Indianapolis, IN: Hackett Publishing Company, 2009).

11 Extract from study of blog posts by Nardon and Aten. See Nardon and Aten "Making Sense of a Foreign Culture through Technology."

12 Bolton, *Reflective Practice.*

13 Julia Cameron, *The Right to Write* (New York: Jeremy P. Tarcher/Putnam, 1998).

14 Philip Robbins and Murat Aydede, "A Short Primer on Situated Cognition," in Philip Robbins and Murat Aydede, eds., *The Cambridge Handbook of Situated Cognition* (Cambridge: Cambridge University Press, 2009).

15 Sunni Brown, *The Doodle Revolution: Unlock the Power to Think Differently* (New York: Portfolio/Penguin, 2014), 24.

16 Gray, "Facilitating Management Learning."

17 David C. Thomas, "Domain and Development of Cultural Intelligence: The Importance of Mindfulness," *Group & Organization Management* 31.1 (2006): 78–99.

18 Bolton *Reflective Practice.*

19 Johns, *Becoming a Reflective Practitioner.*

20 I have explored the process of learning on the fly in detail in the article Luciara Nardon and Richard M. Steers, "The New Global Manager: Learning Cultures on the Fly," *Organizational Dynamics* 37.1 (2008): 47–59.

Chapter 3. Situating Intercultural Interactions

1 Terry O'Reilly, *The Age of Persuasion: Context*. Podcast audio. 27:29. Accessed 8 April 2010 from: http://www.cbc.ca/ageofpersuasion/episode/2010/03/22/season-4-context/.

2 Walter Mishel and Yuichi Shoda, "The Situated Person," in Batja Mesquita, Lisa Fedlamn Barrett, and Eliot R. Smith, eds., *Mind in Context*, 149–73 (New York: Guilford Press, 2010).

3 Eliot R. Smith and Elizabeth C. Collins, "Situated Cognition," in Batja Mesquita, Lisa Fedlamn Barrett, and Eliot R. Smith, eds., *Mind in Context*, 126–48 (New York: Guilford Press, 2010).

4 I draw on the work of organizational scholar Karl Weick on sensemaking. For Weick, sensemaking has seven main characteristics: it is grounded in identity construction, retrospective, enactive of sensible environments, social, ongoing, focused on and by extracted cues, and driven by plausibility rather than accuracy. Readers interested in sensemaking are referred to his book: Karl Weick, *Sensemaking in Organizations* (Thousand Oaks, CA: Sage Publications, 1995).

5 Luciara Nardon, Kathryn Aten, and Daniel Gulanowski. "Expatriate Adjustment in the Digital Age: The Co-creation of Online Social Support Resources through Blogging," *International Journal of Intercultural Relations* 47 (2015): 41–55.

6 Weick, *Sensemaking in Organizations*, 15.

7 The communication process was presented in detail in Luciara Nardon, Richard Steers, and Carlos Sanchez-Runde, "Seeking Common Ground: Strategies for Enhancing Multicultural Communication," *Organizational Dynamics* 40.2 (2011): 85–95.

8 Weick, *Sensemaking in Organizations*; Linda Smircich, and Charles Stubbart "Strategic Management in an Enacted World," *Academy of Management Review* (1985): 724–36.

9 Weick, *Sensemaking in Organizations*.
10 Barbara Czarniawska-Joerges, *Exploring Complex Organizations: A Cultural Perspective* (Newbury Park, CA: Sage, 1992), 34.
11 Gregory Z. Bedny and David Meister, "Theory of Activity and Situation Awareness," *International Journal of Cognitive Ergonomics* 3.1 (1999): 63–72.
12 Several authors have recognized the importance of situations in influencing cognition. Some prominent examples are Kimberley D. Elsbach, Pamela S. Barr, and Andrew B. Hargadon, "Identifying Situated Cognition in Organizations," *Organization Science* 16.4 (2005): 422; Teresa K. Lant, "Organizational Cognition and Interpretation," in Joel A.C. Baum, ed., *The Blackwell Companion to Organizations*, 344–62 (Oxford: Blackwell, 2002); Paul DiMaggio, "Culture and Cognition," *Annual Review of Sociology* 23.1 (1997): 263–87; William Ocasio, "Towards an Attention-Based View of the Firm," *Strategic Management Journal* 18 (1997): 187–206.
13 Robert B. Cialdini, Raymond R. Reno, and Carl A. Kallgren, "A Focus Theory of Normative Conduct: Recycling the Concepts of Norms to Reduce Littering in Public Places," *Journal of Personality and Social Psychology* 58.6 (1990): 1015–26.
14 Tanya L. Chartrand and John A. Bargh, "The Chameleon Effect: The Perception-Behavior Link and Social Interaction," *Journal of Personality and Social Psychology* 76 (1999): 893–910.
15 Sam Sommers, *Situations Matter: Understanding How Context Transforms Your World* (New York: Riverhead Books, 2011).
16 Adam Alter, "When in Chinatown, You Really Do Think More Chinese," *Harvard Business Review* (March 2013), 1–3: https://hbr.org/2013/03/when-in-chinatown-you-really-do-think-more-chinese.
17 Vas Taras, Piers Steel, and Bradley L. Kirkman, "Three Decades of Research on National Culture in the Workplace: Do the Differences Still Make a Difference?" *Organizational Dynamics* 40 (2011): 189–98.
18 Susana Costa e Silva and Luciara Nardon, "An Exploratory Study of Cultural Differences and Perceptions of Relational Risk," in Grazia D. Santangelo and Maryann Feldman, eds., *New Perspectives in International Business Research (Progress in International Business Research, Volume 3)*, 41–58 (Bingley, UK: Emerald Group Publishing Limited, 2008).

Chapter 4. Understanding Culture

1 Based on a search on 22 November 2014.
2 A review of the literature on societal culture suggested that in 1952 there were 164 distinct definitions of culture, and that number has increased significantly since then. See Taras, Vas, Julie Rowney, and Piers Steel, "Half a Century of Measuring Culture: Review of Approaches, Challenges, and

Limitations Based on the Analysis of 121 Instruments for Quantifying Culture," *Journal of International Management* 15.4 (2009): 357–73. The referred study in 1952 is Alfred L. Kroeber and Clyde Kluckhohn, *Culture: A Critical Review of Concepts and Definitions* (New York: Vintage Books, 1952).

3 Nancy J. Adler, John L. Graham, and Theodore S. Gehrke, "Business Negotiations in Canada, Mexico, and the United States," *Journal of Business Research* 15.5 (1987): 411–29; Wendi L. Adair, Tetsushi Okumura, and Jeanne M. Brett, "Negotiation Behavior When Cultures Collide: The United States and Japan," *Journal of Applied Psychology* 86.3 (2001): 371.

4 John W. Berry, "Acculturation: Living Successfully in Two Cultures," *International Journal of Intercultural Relations* 29.6 (2005): 697–712.

5 Management and cognition researchers suggest that the importance of context is due to the situated nature of our cognitions. For more details see Kimberly D. Elsbach, Pamela S. Barr, and Andrew B. Hargadon, "Identifying Situated Cognition in Organizations," *Organization Science* 16.4 (2005): 422; Theresa K. Lant, *Organizational Cognition and Interpretation* (Oxford: Blackwell, 2002), 344–62; William Ocasio, "Towards an Attention-Based View of the Firm," *Strategic Management Journal* 18 (1997): 187–206.

6 Ann Swidler, "Culture in Action: Symbols and Strategies," *American Sociological Review* 51.2 (1986): 273.

7 Swidler, "Culture in Action"; Luciara Nardon and Kathryn Aten, "Beyond a Better Mousetrap: A Cultural Analysis of the Adoption of Ethanol in Brazil," *Journal of World Business* 43.3 (2008): 261–73; Paul DiMaggio, "Culture and Cognition," *Annual Review of Sociology* 23.1 (1997): 263–87.

8 Susan Schneider and Jean-Louis Barsoux, *Managing across Cultures* (London: Financial Times/Prentice Hall, 2003).

9 Ann Swidler, *Talk of Love: How Culture Matters* (Chicago: University of Chicago Press, 2001).

10 Kwok Leung and Michael W. Morris, "Values, Schemas, and Norms in the Culture-Behavior Nexus: A Situated Dynamics Framework," *Journal of International Business Studies* 46 (2015): 1028–50.

11 The exact number of countries varies depending on who is counting. There are 193 UN members and two observer states, Palestine and Vatican State. Political Geography Now (http://www.polgeonow.com/2011/04/how-many-countries-are-there-in-world.html) identifies six additional countries with partial recognition in which some countries recognize their sovereignty but others do not (Taiwan, Western Sahara, Kosovo, South Ossetia, Abkhazia, and Northern Cyprus) and an additional three to six unrecognized de facto sovereign states. Including those, the number of countries could be as high as 207.

12 The ethnologue is the most extensive catalogue of world languages. In February 2015 it was estimated that there are 7,102 living languages, but, of those, 2,447 languages are either dying or in trouble. Ethnologue, Languages of the World. Accessed 5 March 2015 from: https://www .ethnologue.com/world.

13 Adapted from Luciara Nardon and Richard M. Steers, "The Culture Theory Jungle: Divergence and Convergence in Models of National Culture," in Rabi S. Bhagat and Richard M. Steers, eds., *Handbook of Culture, Work, and Organizations*, 3–22 (Cambridge: Cambridge University Press, 2011), 10.

14 Example from Jennifer Nagel, *Knowledge: A Very Short Introduction* (Oxford: Oxford University Press, 2014), 93–4.

15 James P. Carse, *Finite and Infinite Games: A Vision of Life as Play and Possibility* (New York: Free Press, 1986).

Chapter 5. Understanding Individual Differences

1 The discussion of personality in this section is based on the work of Prof. Brian R. Little. Brian R. Little, *Me, Myself, and Us: The Science of Personality and the Art of Well-Being* (New York: HarperCollins Publishers Ltd, 2014).

2 Ibid.

3 Susan Cain, in her bestselling book, has argued eloquently that North Americans undervalue introverts and overvalue extroverts. Susan Cain, *Quiet: The Power of Introverts in a World That Can't Stop Talking* (New York: Random House, 2012).

4 This framework builds on the work of J.W. Berry on acculturation strategies of ethnocultural groups. In the original framework, Berry identified a fourth strategy, marginalization, which occurs when ethnocultural groups let go of their original culture but fail to integrate with dominant groups. John W. Berry, "Acculturation: Living Successfully in Two Cultures," *International Journal of Intercultural Relations* 29.6 (2005): 697–712.

5 Little, *Me, Myself, and Us*.

6 For an example of this approach to intercultural competence development see P. Christopher Earley and Elaine Mosakowski, "Cultural Intelligence," *Harvard Business Review* (2004): 139–46.

7 Eliot R. Smith and Elizabeth C. Collings, "Situated Cognition," in Bajta Mesquita, Lisa F. Barrett, and Eliot R. Smith, eds., *The Mind in Context*, 126–45 (New York: The Guilford Press, 2010).

8 Kathryn Aten, Luciara Nardon, and Diane Isabelle, "Making Sense of Foreign Context: Skilled Migrant's Perceptions of Contextual Barriers and Career Options," *International Journal of Cross-Cultural Management* 16.2 (2016): 191–214.

9 Douglas Stone, Bruce Patton, and Sheila Heen, *Difficult Conversations: How to Discuss What Matters Most* (London: Penguin Books, 2010).

10 Ibid.

11 I had the privilege of taking several classes with Peter Drucker during MBA studies at Claremont Graduate School. A summary of his ideas can be found at Peter Drucker, "Managing Oneself," *Harvard Business Review, Best of HBR 1999* 2.11 (2005): 2–11.

12 David Gray identifies these outcomes as a result of engaging in critical reflection. Intercultural competence development requires critical reflection and, as such, is likely to cause the same emotional disruptions. David E. Gray, "Facilitating Management Learning – Developing Critical Reflection through Reflective Tools," *Management Learning* 38.5 (2007): 495–517.

13 Adapted from David A. Whetten and Kim S. Cameron, *Developing Management Skills* (Upper Saddle River, NJ: Pearson, 2010), 535–6.

Chapter 6. Understanding Situations

1 From an interview at *National Geographic Kids,* May 2009. Accessed 2 August 2016 from: http://admin.wpf.test.nationalgeographic.com/kids/stories/peopleplaces/meet-the-dalai-lama/.

2 The discussion on situational strength draws on the review and synthesis proposed by Meyer and colleagues. Rustin D. Meyer, Reeshad S. Dalal, and Richard Hermida, "A Review and Synthesis of Situational Strength in the Organizational Sciences," *Journal of Management* (2010): 121–40.

3 Ibid.

4 Ibid.

5 Harry C. Triandis, "The Many Dimensions of Culture," *Academy of Management Executive* 18.1 (2004): 88–93.

6 Nanette Fondas and Rosemary Stewart, "Enactment in Managerial Jobs: A Role Analysis," *Journal of Management Studies* 31.1 (1994): 83–103.

7 This example was adapted from Richard M. Steers and Luciara Nardon, *Managing in the Global Economy* (New York: ME Sharpe Inc., 2006), 241–8.

8 William Ocasio, "Towards an Attention-Based View of the Firm," *Strategic Management Journal* 18 (1997): 187–206.

9 Kimberly D. Elsbach and Beth A. Bechkly, "It's More Than a Desk: Working Smarter through Leveraged Office Design," *California Management Review* 49.2 (2007): 80–101.

10 Edward Hall, "A System for the Notation of Proxemics Behavior," *American Anthropologist* 65.5 (1963): 1003–26.

11 Brian R. Little, *Me, Myself, and Us: The Science of Personality and the Art of Well-being* (New York: HarperCollins Publishers Ltd, 2014).

12 This debate is well summarized in Joseph Shaules, *The Intercultural Mind: Connecting Culture, Cognition and Global Living* (Boston, MA: Intercultural Press, 2015), 23–33.

13 Stanley G. Harris, "Organizational Culture and Individual Sensemaking: A Schema-Based Perspective," *Organization Science* 5.3 (1994): 309–21.

14 This passage was used in experiments conducted by Bransford and Johnson investigating the importance of contextual knowledge for comprehension and recall. John D. Bransford and Marcia K. Johnson, "Contextual Prerequisites for Understanding: Some Investigations of Comprehension and Recall," *Journal of Verbal Learning and Verbal Behavior* 11 (1972): 717–26.

15 Harris, "Organizational Culture and Individual Sensemaking."

16 C. Page Moreau, Donald Lehmann, and Arthur B. Markman, "Entrenched Knowledge Structures and Consumer Response to New Products," *Journal of Marketing Research* 38.1 (2001): 14–29.

17 Karl E. Weick, *Sensemaking in Organizations* (Thousand Oaks, CA: Sage Publications, 1995).

18 Tim Hallett, "Symbolic Power and Organizational Culture," *Sociological Theory* 21.2 (2003): 128–49.

19 This model builds on a framework presented in Richard M. Steers, Luciara Nardon, and Carlos Sanchez-Runde, *Management across Cultures: Developing Global Competencies*, 2nd ed. (Cambridge: Cambridge University Press, 2013). The original framework builds on the work of Professor Rosemary Stewart: Rosemary Stewart, *Choices for the Manager* (Englewood Cliffs, NJ: Prentice Hall, 1982).

Chapter 7. Managing Feelings

1 Young Yun Kim, "Intercultural Personhood: Globalization and a Way of Being," *International Journal of Intercultural Relations* 32.4 (2008): 359–68.

2 Daniel Goleman, *Emotional Intelligence* (New York: Bantam, 1995), quoted in Edward W. Taylor, "Transformative Learning Theory: A Neurobiological Perspective of the Role of Emotions and Unconscious Ways of Knowing," *International Journal of Lifelong Education* 20.3 (2001): 218–36.

3 William B. Gudykunst, *Bridging Differences: Effective Intergroup Communication* (Thousand Oaks, CA: Sage, 1998); Miriam Sobre-Denton and Daniel Hart, "Mind the Gap: Application-Based Analysis of Cultural Adjustment Models," *International Journal of Intercultural Relations* 32.6 (2008): 538–52.

4 Gudykunst, *Bridging Differences*.

5 Taylor, "Transformative Learning Theory."

6 Douglas Stone, Bruce Patton, and Sheila Heen, *Difficult Conversations: How to Discuss What Matters Most* (London: Penguin Books, 2010).

 7 The Center for Nonviolent Communication, *Feelings Inventory*. Accessed
    2 January 2017 from: https://www.cnvc.org/Training/feelings-inventory.
 8 Antonio Damasio and Gil B. Carvalho, "The Nature of Feelings: Evolu-
    tionary and Neurobiological Origins," *Nature Reviews Neuroscience* 14.2
    (2013): 143–52.
 9 Kerry Patterson, Joseph Grenny, Ron McMillan, and Al Switzler, *Crucial
    Conversations: Tools for Talking When Stakes Are High* (New York: McGraw
    Hill, 2012).
10 Yuri Miyamoto and Carol D. Ryff, "Cultural Differences in the Dialectical
    and Non-dialectical Emotional Styles and Their Implications for Health,"
    Cognition and Emotion 25.1 (2011): 22–39.
11 Christina Kotchemidova, "Emotion Culture and Cognitive Constructions
    of Reality," *Communication Quarterly* 58.2 (2010): 207–34.
12 Erving Goffman, *Interaction Ritual: Essays on Face-to-Face Behavior* (Garden
    City, NY: Doubleday, 1967).
13 Christopher K. Germer, *The Mindful Path to Self-compassion: Freeing Yourself
    from Destructive Thoughts and Emotions* (New York: The Guilford Press, 2009).
14 Ibid., 72; J. David Creswell, Baldwin M. Way, Naomi I. Eisenberger, and
    Matthew D. Lieberman, "Neural Correlates of Dispositional Mindfulness
    during Affect Labeling," *Psychosomatic Medicine* 69.6 (2007): 560–5.
15 Carolus Van Nijnatten, "Finding the Words: Social Work from a Develop-
    mental Perspective," *Journal of Social Work Practice* 20.2 (2006): 133–44.
16 Terrance L. Albrecht and Madelaine B. Adelman, *Communicating Social
    Support* (Thousand Oaks, CA: Sage, 1987), cited in Madelaine B. Adelman,
    "Cross-cultural Adjustment: A Theoretical Perspective on Social Support,"
    International Journal of Intercultural Relations 12.3 (1988): 189.
17 Julia Cameron, *The Right to Write: An Invitation and Initiation into the Writing
    Life* (Los Angeles: Tarcher, 1999).
18 Donald Altman, *The Mindfulness Code: Keys for Overcoming Stress, Anxiety,
    Fear and Unhappiness* (Novato, CA: New World Library, 2010).
19 Stone, Patton, and Heen, *Difficult Conversations*.
20 Ibid.
21 Barbara Fredrickson, *Positivity: Top-Notch Research Reveals the Upward Spiral
    That Will Change Your Life* (New York: Harmony, 2009).
22 Stone, Patton, and Heen, *Difficult Conversations*.

Chapter 8. Communicating across Cultures

 1 The topic of difficult communication has been explored in detail in the
    following two books: Douglas Stone, Bruce Patton, and Sheila Heen,
    Difficult Conversations: How to Discuss What Matters Most (London: Penguin

Books, 2010); see also Kerry Patterson, Joseph Grenny, Ron McMillan, and Al Switzler, *Crucial Conversations: Tools for Talking When Stakes Are High* (New York: McGraw Hill, 2012).

2 Herbert H. Clark, *Using Language* (Cambridge: Cambridge University Press, 1996); Herbert H. Clark and Susan E. Brennan, "Grounding in Communication," *Perspectives on Socially Shared Cognition* 13 (1991): 127–49.

3 Joseph Shaules, *The Intercultural Mind: Connecting Culture, Cognition and Global Living* (Boston, MA: Intercultural Press, 2015), 160.

4 Ibid.

5 The communication process was presented in detail in Luciara Nardon, Richard Steers, and Carlos Sanchez-Runde, "Seeking Common Ground: Strategies for Enhancing Multicultural Communication," *Organizational Dynamics* 40.2 (2011): 85–95.

6 Ibid.

7 This quotation as well as other blog quotations cited in this book were identified through a large study I conducted with my colleague Kathryn Aten. We analyzed 606 blog posts written by expatriates and immigrants living in Canada to understand their adjustment experience. This quotation was presented at the EGOS 2015 colloquium.

8 Luciara Nardon and Kathryn Aten, "Making Sense of a Foreign Culture through Technology: Triggers, Mechanisms, and Introspective Focus in Newcomers' Blog Narratives," *International Journal of Intercultural Relations* 54 (2016): 15–20.

9 Edward T. Hall and Mildred Reed Hall, *Understanding Cultural Differences: Germans, French and Americans* (Yarmouth, ME: Intercultural Press, 1990).

10 Larry A. Samovar, Richard E. Porter, and Edwin R. McDaniel, *Communication between Cultures* (Belmont, CA: Wadsworth Publishing, 2012).

11 Clark, *Using Language*.

12 Stone, Patton, and Heen, *Difficult Conversations*.

13 Patterson, Grenny, McMillan, and Switzler, *Crucial Conversations*.

14 Victor J. Friedman and Ariane Berthoin Antal, "Negotiating Reality: A Theory of Action Approach to Intercultural Competence,"*Management Learning* 36 (2005): 69–86; Luciara Nardon and Richard M. Steers, "The New Global Manager: Learning Cultures on the Fly," *Organizational Dynamics* 37.1 (2008): 47–59.

15 Stone, Patton, and Heen, *Difficult Conversations*.

16 Linda Hill, *Building Effective One-on-One Work Relationships* (Watertown, MA: Harvard Business Publishing, 1996).

17 The following discussion draws on Carlos Sanchez-Runde, Luciara Nardon, and Richard M. Steers, "The Cultural Roots of Ethical Conflicts in Global Business," *Journal of Business Ethics* 16.4 (2013): 689–701.

18 Anne Donnellon, Barbara Gray, and Michel G. Bougon, "Communication, Meaning, and Organized Action," *Administrative Science Quarterly* (1986): 43–55.

19 Stone and colleagues provide a detailed explanation of how people can communicate about disagreements. See Stone, Patton, and Heen, *Difficult Conversations*, 151.

20 Based on Chris Argyris and Donald A. Schon, *Organizational Learning II: Theory, Method, and Practice* (Reading, MA: Addison-Wesley, 1986).

Chapter 9. Moving Forward

1 John Suler, *Zen Stories to Tell Your Neighbors* (Doylestown, PA: True Center Publishing, 1986–present). Accessed on 28 November 2015 from: www .arvindguptatoys.com/arvindgupta/zen-for-neighbours.pdf.

2 G.P. Hodgkinson and M.P. Healey, "Coming in from the Cold: The Psychological Foundations of Radical Innovation Revisited," *Industrial Marketing Management* 43.8 (2014): 1306–13.

3 Ray Bradbury, *Zen in the Art of Writing: Essays on Creativity* (Santa Barbara, CA: Joshua Odell Editions, 1994), 145.

4 Joseph Shaules, *The Intercultural Mind: Connecting Culture, Cognition, and Global Living* (Boston, MA: Intercultural Press, 2015), 23.

5 Ibid.

6 This section draws on my research with Kathryn Aten: Kathryn Aten and Luciara Nardon, "Intercultural Competence in the Digital Age," presented at the Academy of International Business Southeast Conference in November 2016.

7 Luciara Nardon, Kathryn Aten, and Daniel Gulanowski, "Expatriate Adjustment in the Digital Age: The Co-creation of Online Social Support Resources through Blogging," *International Journal of Intercultural Relations* 47 (2015): 41–55.

Appendix A. Cross-cultural Studies

1 Samuel A. Stouffer and Jackson Toby, "Role Conflict and Personality," *American Journal of Sociology* 56.5 (1951): 395–406.

2 Clyde Kluckhohn, "Values and Value Orientations in the Theory of Action," in T. Parsons and E.A. Shils, eds., *Towards a General Theory of Action* (Cambridge, MA: Harvard University Press, 1951); Florence Kluckhohn and F. Strodtbeck, *Variations in Value Orientations* (Evanston, IL: Row, Peterson, 1961).

3 Geert Hofstede, *Culture's Consequences: Comparing Values, Behaviors, Institutions, and Organizations across Nations* (Thousand Oaks, CA: Sage Publications, 1980).

4 Shalom Schwartz, "Universals in the Content and Structure of Values: Theoretical Advances and Empirical Tests in 20 Countries," in Mark Zanna, ed., *Advances in Experimental Social Psychology,* 1–65 (New York: Academic Press, 1992).

5 Edward T. Hall, *The Silent Language* (New York: Doubleday, 1959); Edward T. Hall and Mildred R. Hall, *Understanding Cultural Differences* (Yarmouth, ME: Intercultural Press, 1990).

6 Fons Trompenaars, *Riding the Waves of Culture: Understanding Cultural Diversity in Business* (London: Economist Books, 1993); Fons Trompenaars and Charles Hampden-Turner, *Riding the Waves of Culture: Understanding Diversity in Global Business* (New York: McGraw Hill, 1998).

7 Robert House, Paul Hanges, Mansour Javidan, Peter Dorfman, and Vipin Gupta, *Culture, Leadership and Organizations: The GLOBE Study of 62 Societies* (Thousand Oaks, CA: Sage Publications, 2004).

8 This sixth dimension was added in 2010 as a result of work conducted in collaboration with Bulgarian sociologist Michael Minkov: see Michael Minkov and Geert Hofstede, "The Evolution of Hofstede's Doctrine," *Cross Cultural Management: An International Journal* 18.1 (2011): 10–20.

Index

Page numbers in italics indicate items in tables.